1-800-AWAY-IRS

The Answer To A Nation's Plea

Strategies To Protect Yourself
Secrets To Save You Thousands

Robert Bennington
&
Cort W. Christie

Griffin Publishing Group
Glendale, California

Disclaimer Notice

While every attempt has been made to provide accurate information within this book, the authors and the National Audit Defense Network will not accept responsibility for any claim, case study or legal situation mentioned herein. The authors have discussed tax issues with former IRS agents and tax professionals for accuracy, but every reader is urged to consult a competent legal professional.

The authors discuss stories of real people who have placed themselves in jeopardy with the IRS or other government officials, and while their stories need to be told, the authors will not be responsible for any information to any person regarding the confidential material in the text. For security reasons, the authors and the National Audit Defense Network are unable to reveal any anonymous sources within the book or provide information for the same.

The National Audit Defense Network has not accepted nor will they accept any individual into the organization who has intentionally deceived the IRS, assuming they have informed NADN of such, and in no way condones or tolerates tax evasion or dishonesty.

Publisher: Robert Howland
Director of Operations: Robin Howland
Managing Editor: Marjorie L. Marks
Cover Design: Mike Berman

10 9 8 7 6 5 4 3 2 1
ISBN 1-882180-97-6

Griffin Publishing Group
544 Colorado Street
Glendale, California 91204

Telephone: (818) 244-1470

ACKNOWLEDGMENTS

We thank the many people who have helped in the making of this book, including our families, who support us every day, even those days when we are working long hours, and who encourage us along the way, never failing to provide both constructive criticism and praise.

Thanks to our creative team at the National Audit Defense Network, who assisted us during the research and writing process. Thank you, Betsy Smith, for your creative ideas and editorial expertise. Your dedication to the book was invaluable! Thank you, Mike Berman, for your promotional ideas and cover design. Thank you Ko Hiashi for your research, both on the Internet and through the library—your expertise was a great asset. Thank you to Gordon Jones for your "Inside Washington" insight into the history of and alternatives to the IRS. Thank you to Lisa Wagner for your editorial style and assistance in pulling together some of our thoughts.

Thank you to Dick Grossman for your vast knowledge of the IRS and your technical expertise, both for the book and for helping our clients every day. Thank you to all of the National Audit Defense Network staff, for your hard work in making our company prosper and putting in all the extra hours we needed in order to grow. Our success as a company is dependent on top notch employees, and we are lucky to have all of you.

We give a special thank you to Mr. Pat Cavanaugh. Without your vision of helping people to successfully defend themselves against the IRS, none of us would be where we are. Thank you, Pat, for all your assistance and mentoring while we have seen NADN prosper.

Of course, a good book is not possible without a good publisher, and Griffin Publishing accepted a challenge and has exceeded our expectations. Thank you Marjie Marks, Robin Howland and Bob Howland of Griffin Publishing Group for your time and effort with this project.

Lastly, we give a special thank you to our members. Your support is the backbone of our organization and without you we would not exist. Thank you!

DEDICATION

TO OUR FAMILIES. NOTHING ELSE IS POSSIBLE WITHOUT
SUPPORT FROM THOSE WE LOVE.

CONTENTS

PREFACE

One of the biggest problems we encountered while researching this book was the secretive nature of IRS agents. We work with hundreds of former agents, and they all respond similarly when asked whether they want to go on record with their statements: "No." Too much to lose, they always say: "We might never be able to survive in the public or private sector if we say the 'wrong' things and it gets back to some mythical beast at 1111 Constitution Avenue."

With no one wishing to go on record to discuss their organization, how can its problems ever be dealt with?

Consequently, we have used several anonymous sources for this book and, even so, have had to be especially careful not to mention the specific geographic location of these agents. We also quoted other media extensively. It is important to note that abuse by the IRS is not a strange or foreign idea left only to conspiracy or anti-government groups. It is a national travesty that agents are given unharnessed power to manipulate, weaken and destroy human beings for a few extra revenue dollars.

A major contributor to our cause is Dr. Arthur Green, a dentist in the Washington DC area. Dr.

Green called our National Audit Defense Network (NADN) offices on Sunday, September 21, 1997 to tell us his story of IRS abuse. The woman who took his phone call was so moved that she told our media director, "This man's story should be heard." The following week, Dr. Green's fourteen-year struggle to maintain his sanity amid IRS liens on his home, his dental practice, his cars, and his income was told on national TV.

NADN helped him deal with the IRS and work out his situation, assisted by one of our staff members, who is a former IRS agent. We take pride in having helped Dr. Green, and look forward to following his story as he once again begins to enjoy a normal life.

No one wants to believe their government is flawed and abusive to its people. Voters can be extremely lenient and protective regarding the behavior of those whom they have elected to represent them because no one wants to admit they made a poor choice. However, the problem at hand with the IRS has become so extreme that even the most guarded public officials admit there is a crisis at 1111 Constitution Avenue.

When ordinary Americans turn in their tax returns on April 15, they do not anticipate the assaults on their patience, their time, or their bank accounts that ensue when they are informed that they will be audited. The only problem more frustrating to taxpayers than being audited is the attitude and often careless behavior of the agent who audits them. Some IRS employees will tell you that there are high satisfaction rates on their surveys. What they don't mention is who exactly receives these surveys and whether such surveys are representative of the taxpayer body as a whole.

IRS bashing is not the purpose of this book, however. Neither the National Audit Defense Network nor the authors wish to sensationalize the problems of this agency. Rather, NADN chooses to bring to light the frustrations of taxpayers who have been treated unfairly by the IRS and its agents. We also issue a call to action to all those who feel as we do—in the hope that collectively we can influence the IRS to change.

Do not sit by and allow your rights as a taxpayer to be taken away. Do not allow Congress or the President to each accuse the other of politicizing the issue, only to avoid making needed changes in the tax code or the IRS. Americans have the power of democracy; we can change what we do not like about our government.

The IRS began with benign intentions: to collect the money that people rightfully owe their government and distribute it to the various govenment agencies that need it to provide services for the American people. And so it went for many years, until the Nixon administration brought to light the terrible tragedies that can occur within the IRS if power is given to the wrong people. For their part, the IRS has experienced more than its share of mishaps; it seems that each time it attempts to improve its operation and/or its image, such as its widely publicized endeavor to upgrade its computer system, the agency creates further complications for itself.

Americans need *800 Away IRS,* a book that reveals truths about the IRS—including the history and mechanics of this secretive agency—that may seem cynical, but which are borne out by the experiences of taxpayers whose stories are included in this book. In addition, *800 Away IRS* shows you how to save taxes.

We believe that an understanding of who and what you are *really* dealing with when you encounter the IRS will allow you to defend yourself more effectively.

With all this in mind, we encourage you to delve into *800 Away IRS* so that when you file your taxes next time, you can expect—perhaps for the first time—to have a positive taxpaying experience.

It's true—you can pay your taxes, get audited and live to tell about it!

CHAPTER ONE

THE IRS MESS

> *"Whenever anyone wants to know what really goes on inside the IRS...IRS higher-ups can cite 'taxpayer privacy' as a way to avoid spilling the beans."*
>
> —Shelley Davis, *Unbridled Power*,
> Harper Business, 1997

In a recent letter to nationally syndicated columnist Ann Landers, a reader wrote:

> You certainly went easy on the Internal Revenue Service in your recent reply to 'Los Angeles Taxpayer.' He described a tale of red-tape madness. You replied, 'It's a miracle the IRS doesn't screw up more often.' Frankly, Ann, you need a reality check on just how incompetent the IRS really is.

> The IRS does screw up more often. How about the 3,000 people notified by the IRS in 1993 that they each owed $4 billion in back taxes? How about the Philadelphia chemical firm that was penalized nearly $47,000 because the IRS determined that its tax payment of $4,448,112.88 was a dime short?

> The IRS recently spent $8 billion to overhaul its computer programs. What it got for all that money, a top official admitted, are systems that 'do not work in the real world.'

The federal tax agency sends out some thirty million penalty notices every year. Nearly half are erroneous.

As the tax deadline approaches each year, the IRS invites taxpayers to call its toll-free number with questions. When they do call in, millions are given the wrong answers. Then when those callers reply on those wrong answers, they are slapped with interest, penalties and liens on their property. The Heritage Foundation compiled nine pages of case examples that underscore IRS ineptitude. Here are just a few of them:

* The number of times the IRS gave the wrong answer in 1993 to taxpayers seeking assistance with their tax forms—8.5 million

* The percentage of its own budget for which the IRS could not account in an audit—64 percent

* The number of correction notices sent out by the IRS each year that turn out to be wrong—five million

* The number of women wrongly fined each year because they get divorced or married—three million

* The number of taxpayers whose old-age benefits will be cut because the IRS doesn't properly record their tax payments—ten million

As the IRS Tax Code grows ever more complex, it becomes easier for agents to find something wrong with any tax return. The existing tax code has become a source of unfathomable power for IRS agents—and that power corrupts. In a survey of IRS officials in 1991, three-fourths said they would probably not be 'completely honest' if they had to testify before Congress. Nearly half admitted they would use their position to harass personal enemies.

So take a few lashes with the wet noodle, Ann. Then add your voice to the cry for a simpler, slimmer, saner tax code."[†]

The letter, signed "Jeff Jacoby, columnist for the *Boston Globe*" received a reply from Ann Landers as follows:

Dear Jeff Jacoby: You've made a pretty solid case against the Internal Revenue Service and knocked some credible holes in what now appears to be my rather lame defense. I'm getting out the wet noodle in anticipation of forty lashes. I found especially unsettling the survey of IRS officials in 1991 who said they probably would not be completely honest if they had to testify before Congress.

If anyone from the IRS would like to respond to Jeff's charges, I will gladly step aside and let him or her use my podium. Any takers?

Not a single IRS official took Ann up on her offer to print his or her side of the story.

Why wouldn't any IRS agent reply? After all, if you are proud of your company and you believe that the principles it stands for are noble, you would defend it from attack. One of the biggest indicators of guilt is silence.

So how did the IRS become so uncontrollable? What happened in this agency's past that turned a once seemingly benign organization into an 800-pound gorilla with no compassion or even practicality when it comes to collecting taxes? The

---

[†] Ann Landers newspaper column on June 22, 1997 in the *San Diego Union-Tribune*. Copyrighted by Creators Syndicate. Letter was signed by Jeff Jacoby, columnist, *Boston Globe*.

answer, not surprisingly, lies within some strategic situations in the IRS's past that have made the agency literally immune from accountability. In order to change this, then, we must study the agency's history.

CHAPTER TWO

A SHORT HISTORY
OF TAXATION

Taxation is as old as government. Every society in recorded history has had some form of ministerial class, and virtually without exception, this class has depended for its maintenance on some form of levy on the membership in the society.

The earliest governments were an extension of the religious organization of the society, with the priest class performing ministerial functions, and perhaps directing military operations. Tithes and offerings characterized the levies in these societies, and these were usually voluntary. The payment would be in kind—grain and cattle—which could be used for the sustenance of the priest-governing class. As recounted in Genesis, the treasuries of the Pharaoh were filled with grain, not gold.

But the appearance of record-keeping of incomes and a levy on incomes was not slow to develop.

By the 1st century B.C., all incomes were registered in China, so that a tax of five percent could be levied. At that, five percent was a bargain. Some oriental despots levied taxes at nearly fifty percent, almost as much as the tax man of today.

A common method of collecting taxes was "tax farming,"a system under which taxes were collected by entrepreneurs licensed to perform this function by the state. They could retain a percentage of collections for themselves, remitting the balance to the higher, licensing authority. The Lord's apostle, Matthew, was such a tax collector.

Some tax farmers were very subtle. The sheriff of Nottingham may have been ham-handed, but by the time of Henry VIII, sophistication was the rule. Consider John Morton, the inventor of "Morton's Fork," an ingenious device for maximizing tax revenues. If Morton saw that a nobleman wasn't spending much, he would deduce that the individual had to have plenty left for the King. If the baron was spending like a drunken sailor, well, obviously he was rich, and so he also had plenty for the King. Either way, the King always won.

TAXATION IN AMERICA

The American Colonies may have had their origins in a struggle for religious freedom, but the United States of America was born out of a tax revolt.

During the colonial period, taxes were levied on goods exported from the colonies. Under Acts of Trade and Navigation, most exports had to go to

English ports, from which they were re-exported to Europe. These taxes were often unfair. For example, a tax of four cents a pound was levied on tobacco at a time when the weed brought less than a penny a pound at wharf side. But since the tariff was incorporated into the selling price of the goods, it was not really paid by the American exporter, but by the English or European customer.

Meanwhile, back at home, Americans were enjoying a life virtually free from governmental interference. Taxes were light (when they were levied at all: for one three-year period, Connecticut levied none) and easily avoided. There were various attempts made to weld the colonies into a cohesive unit, under a government that would have taxing authority, but none of these plans came to fruition, because the colonies would not give up their independent powers. These freedoms were bought at some considerable cost to the British Government, which was put to the expense of defending the colonies through the French and Indian Wars, Pontiac's Rebellion, and the War of Jenkins Ear and other military exercises. The colonies closest to the actual battles did contribute, but the Middle Colonies were getting a free ride, especially Pennsylvania, with its Quaker pacifism. Burdened with war debt, George III and his ministers from 1763 forward sought a way to recoup losses, and it was this effort to levy taxes directly on the colonists that led to the War of Independence.

The first step was the tightening of customs duties by the Revenue Act of 1764, mainly on sugar and molasses, but also including other goods such as silk and wine. Although the purpose of this Act was to raise revenue rather than to regulate trade, it was still within the traditional framework of taxation. It was still an *external* tax.

But the Stamp Act of 1765 was a radical departure. A tax on virtually all legal documents, printed matter, and playing cards, this was a heavy tax indeed, and one that had to be paid in sterling, rather than colonial currencies. It was, furthermore, an *internal* tax, and as such was held by the colonists to be illegal.

The colonists would not bear this burden. The reaction was immediate and universal throughout the colonies. The stamped paper was confiscated and burned by mobs (called the Sons of Liberty by a British parliamentarian), and the British governors were harassed and abused. This united and violent action completely nullified the Act, and no further efforts were made to enforce it. It further resulted in the Stamp Act Congress, a movement toward unity in the colonies to which nine colonies responded by meeting in New York City. The Stamp Act was repealed a year later, but at the same time Parliament declared its right to tax the colonies.

The Townshend Acts were the next step, passed in 1767 and remaining in force for three years. They constituted taxes on trade, but they also included a tightened administration of anti-smuggling laws, and better collection of duties. They were an onerous burden on the colonies, but were constitutional according to colonial thought and custom. They did raise considerable money, even though they were imposed at a time when trade was depressed.

And they provoked a non-importation movement, or boycott, of the taxed goods, to the point that the Acts contributed to the fall of the British government in 1770 and their repeal (except for the tax on tea, which was kept in order to enshrine the principle of British supremacy). The result was the Boston Tea Party, matched by similar rebellions against the tea tax in the Middle and Southern Colonies. The Tea Party incited the British government to direct action, and thus led directly to the War of Independence.

While the Revolutionary War settled the issue of British taxation of America, it also set the stage for the next round of battles over taxation. The revolt against taxation that led to the independence of the colonies was directly responsible for the failure of the first efforts to unite them. Under the Articles of Confederation, the central government had no power of taxation, not even the power to tax imports. The Continental Congress could assess the states a proportion of the federal expenses based on the total value of land within the states, but the states themselves had to levy the taxes and remit them. Naturally, contributions were never as much as the central government thought it needed, and the inclusion of a taxing power was an important part of the Constitution of the United States.

As an aside, it might be worth noting that the complaints of the central government under the

Articles of Confederation were precisely the same as the complaints we now hear from the international bureaucrats at the United Nations. Again today, "assessments" are made to member states, but there is no enforcement mechanism if those states do not pay those assessments. And the United Nations is seeking a source of income that does not depend on voluntary action of member states. An international carbon tax has been suggested, as has a tax on international travel, international business transactions and international communications.

In the colonial period in America, there was a centripetal force driving the colonies together into that federal union: the basic homogeneity of the society. That homogeneity is not present at the United Nations, and for that reason it is unlikely that the United Nations will follow the pattern set by the evolution from confederation to federal union, with a strong taxing power, but the possibility is there, and it is certain that internationalists would like to see the same development.

In Article I, Sec. 8, the 1787 Constitution of the United States empowered the Congress to "lay and collect taxes, duties, imposts and excises...but all duties, imposts and excises shall be uniform throughout the United States." This general power was limited by Sec. 9, which states that "No capitation, or other direct, tax shall be laid, unless in proportion to the census of enumeration herein directed to be taken."

While it may seem obvious to us that an income tax would be a "direct tax," it is not clear that that is what the Founding Fathers meant by the term. Indeed, it is not clear what was meant. During the Debates at the Constitutional Convention, a delegate asked what "direct taxes" meant, and got no answer.

In any event, the need for revenue so drove official thinking, including that of the judiciary, that by the end of the Civil War, the term "direct taxes" had come to mean only capitation taxes, and taxes on land.

Many seem to believe today that the repeal of the Sixteenth Amendment would end the power of the federal government to levy an income tax. Our constitutional history does not bear out this belief. The courts simply defined many kinds of taxes, including a general tax on income, as "excise taxes," permitted under the Constitution. The 1881 ease of *Springer v. U.S.* (102 U.S. 586) specifically upholds the constitutionality of an income tax.

It is true that in the 1895 case of *Pollock v. Farmers Loan and Trust* (157 U.S. 429 and 158 U.S. 601) the Supreme Court struck down the Income Tax Act of 1894. It is on that decision that opponents of the Sixteenth Amendment rely for their belief that its repeal would end forever the income tax.

But again, even as during the Civil War and the immediate postwar period, the government's need for money controlled policy, even constitutional law. Following the *Pollock* decision, the Court again chipped away at the limitation on the taxing power.

By the time of the adoption of the Sixteenth Amendment in 1913, whether by inventive definitions and redefinitions of the term "direct tax," or by a resort to the pre-*Pollock* history of the excise tax, the government had recovered most of its power to tax incomes.

The Sixteenth Amendment was a direct result of the *Pollock* decision, and it did indeed make a reversal of *Pollock* unnecessary. But such a reversal was inevitable by decisions of the Court, whether explicit or *sub silentio*.

This constitutional history is important for the debate over tax reform, discussed in Chapter 15. Advocates of the national sales tax propose an accompanying repeal of the Sixteenth Amendment, and opponents of the NST vow that it can be accepted only if accompanied by such a repeal. History suggests that even repeal will not be enough, and that a better mechanism for controlling the tax appetite of government must be found— perhaps through a requirement that it take a supermajority to raise taxes. Congress already has voted upon, though not passed, such a measure, an example of which is contained in the best of the Balanced Budget Constitutional Amendments (the Barton-Kyl Bill). A version of this super-majority requirement is contained in the Armey-Shelby Flat Tax Bill, but as a statute it would always be subject to reversal by simple majority. And, in fact, a clever parliamentarian can get around any such supermajority requirement by a simple majority anyway.

In any event, following adoption of the Sixteenth Amendment, Congress did enact a tax on both individual and corporate income. The income tax has been progressive from the beginning. To start with, it exempted the first $3,000 of income for a single person, and the first $4,000 for a married couple. These exemptions removed 98 percent of the population from the tax rolls. Tax rates rose from an initial 1 percent to a high of 7 percent.

The fiscal requirements of World War I drove the next round of tax increases, in both rates and coverage. During the war, the exemptions were cut in half, bringing many more people under taxation, perhaps as much as 15 percent of the work force. The rates also were sharply increased, to a high of 77 percent for individuals and 64 percent for corporations. Following the war, both rates and coverage declined again, but World War II permanently established taxation as a fact of life for the vast majority of Americans.

The number of workers covered reached 90 percent during the War, and the marginal tax rate (for incomes of more than $200,000) was 94 percent. During this period, the payroll tax also assumed importance with the financing of the Social Security System.

Following World War II, tax law remained relatively stable (with one tax cut and then a small spike to pay for the Korean War) until 1962. Individual exemptions were set at $600 per person, and the top marginal individual rate was 91 percent, on taxable income of more than $400,000.

As a practical matter, because of a proliferation of deductions and exemptions, the 91 percent rate affected very few people.

Beginning in 1963 (the famous Kennedy Tax Cuts beloved of Supply Side economists), Congress enacted a series of tax cuts, which were financed by the bracket creep produced by higher inflation and an unindexed tax code. As individual incomes were artificially inflated, taxpayers were pushed into higher tax brackets; tax rates could then be cut without significantly reducing government revenues. This game was played repeatedly until the election of Ronald Reagan in 1980. His first tax bill of 1981 indexed tax brackets, ending the game. Coupled with the flattening of rates and the elimination of many exemptions and deductions in 1986, the Reagan tax policies produced the strongest resistance ever to a progressive tax code, and fueled the tax revolt that still is going on.

The period between Kennedy and Reagan also saw the vastly increased use of the tax code to produce and discourage specific kinds of economic (or even social) activity. Obviously, the complication of the tax code was as important as its absolute burden in generating antipathy to the collecting agency, the Internal Revenue Service. Given the job of monitoring social and economic activity, as well as simply raising revenue, the IRS acquired enormous powers, powers whose abuse was felt by virtually every citizen, and which was so graphically shown at congressional hearings in September 1997.

The Reagan years witnessed another phenomenon, brought about by the addition of the Medicare health insurance scheme to the existing Social Security System. Both of these are financed by payroll taxes, and after Social Security shifted away from a strictly "pay as you go" approach in 1983, in the direction of (but not yet reaching) a funded retirement program, the payroll tax burden spiked upward. Coupled with the indexation of personal exemptions proposed by Ronald Reagan and enacted during his first term, these developments caused millions of taxpayers to pay more in payroll taxes than in income taxes. This burden is all the more onerous in view of the fact that few of those currently paying these payroll taxes expect to get much out of the systems, and the reality that for those now entering the work force, the "investment" they are making in these systems will produce a negative return.

The popular perception is that the 1981 Reagan tax cuts (the Supply Side cuts) produced the horrendous budget deficits of the 1980s. The reality is that while revenues dipped slightly immediately following the cuts, they more than doubled during the Reagan years, as the incentive effects of lower marginal rates stimulated the economic activity promised. On average, federal revenues increased by about $90 billion a year over the eight years of the Reagan presidency. The problem was that the Democratic Congress spent every new nickel, and another dime besides.

The deficits produced different schemes for getting deficits under control, from the Gramm-

Rudman-Hollings Act to the George Bush-Dick Darman Budget Deal of 1991, which cost Bush the election of 1992, and delivered us to the tender ministrations of Bill Clinton. Clinton's first action was to enact the largest tax increase in history (in the words of Democrat Sen. Pat Moynihan of New York). While the Clinton increase has not produced the economic debacle Republicans warned about, neither has it ushered in an economic Nirvana. Economic growth has been steady, but it has been far from spectacular. Most analysts give the credit to Federal Reserve Board Chairman Alan Greenspan, for keeping to a slow and steady growth in the money supply.

The tax burden on individuals remains high, and the pressures for real relief remain powerful. Even more important to individual Americans than the cost of the system is its complexity, leading to the movement for total overhaul, and the abolition of the IRS, as discussed in the following chapters.

CHAPTER THREE

WHO IS TODAY'S

IRS AGENT

& WHY DOES HE BELIEVE YOU ARE GUILTY UNTIL PROVEN INNOCENT?

You cannot help the poor by destroying the rich. You cannot lift the wage earner by pulling down the wage payer.

—Abraham Lincoln

If Patrick Henry thought that taxation without representation was bad, he should see how bad it is with representation.

—*Old Farmer's Almanac*

A former IRS agent told NADN recently that the typical revenue collector is just like the California coyote. The California coyote has caused quite a ruckus in residential neighborhoods. The animals have been rummaging through trash cans, wandering around backyards and harassing and even eating family pets throughout Southern California.

Outraged, some counties decided to plant traps to catch and kill the coyotes. The project succeeded in only one aspect: self-imposed Darwinism. Naive coyotes were caught immediately. Resourceful coyotes saw what happened to members of their packs and stealthily walked around the traps. Thus, the smart coyotes reproduced and taught their litters to avoid the traps also. California homeowners ended up doing themselves a greater disservice than they imagined.

The moral of the story, ironically, lies within our tax system. IRS revenue agents are the coyotes of the tax system. Agents who see the pain that tax collecting can bring, who sympathize with the taxpayers who do everything they can to be good Americans, are caught in the sympathy trap and eventually lose or leave the job. Those revenue agents who truly enjoy making peoples' lives difficult, who seek out tax returns with which to find fault, have walked around the sympathy trap. They're hungry enough that the implications of what they do have no consequence for them. Like the smart coyotes, eventually they will teach new agents, who will be even hungrier than they are. What's left is a revenue collector with little compassion.

The same former agent said that there is an evolutionary process to the nastiness of some revenue collectors:

"Make no mistake, the coyote agents are good at what they do, based on the big revenue they bring into the agency. But when you get right down to it, they are probably agents because they couldn't get a job on Wall Street or with a CPA firm. We're not talking about selfless civil servants here.

"Keep in mind also that there is an overwhelming inferiority complex among revenue agents. Oftentimes, they are fighting tax preparers who drive better cars, live in better houses, and wear better clothes than they do."

Understanding the mentality of the average IRS revenue agent is key to understanding the whole tax system. When you know the way IRS agents are trained and their mentality about tax-collecting, then you know how the IRS works, and you know what you are up against every April and the best way to prepare for it.

Max†, a former IRS agent and accountant who is now out of the business, told NADN how the IRS trains its employees to assume that taxpayers are guilty until proven innocent.

"When IRS agents receive the cases that have been chosen for auditing, they immediately research them to see what is wrong with them. The

---

† Max is a pseudonym; the former agent wishes to remain anonymous for security reasons.

agent just *knows* that something must be wrong with the return; they never assume that a taxpayer was honest or that the return doesn't have a mistake on it. That's just not an option."

According to the article, "Our Public Servants at Work," which appeared in the *Wall Street Journal* in April 1997, "IRS auditors are rewarded based on how much additional taxes they impose on people, not on whether they follow the law."

A report in the April 1997 issue of "Inc." Magazine revealed that clients of some tax experts have been bullied even when their meticulous documentation shows they are innocent. One client discussed in the article had been questioned on purchases of $2 or less. The federal tax on a $2 deduction would have been less than eighty cents.

When you realize that you are presumed guilty before the audit even begins, you become equipped with the best weapon you can have—anger. Most people panic when they receive notice of an audit. They also feel helpless. It is a big mystery how a government agency such as the IRS can adopt a policy of assuming that someone is guilty until proven innocent without receiving an outcry from the public.

Envision this scenario: An accused criminal in a court of law was told that she would go to jail unless she could conclusively prove beyond any doubt that she did not commit the crime. She cannot prove that she did not commit the crime she is accused of, because she was the only person at the scene of the "crime." You are outraged and protest the woman's conviction. The judge of the woman's case decides to put you in jail, because you must be guilty of something, or you wouldn't protest her decision. Because you can't prove that you didn't do anything, and because no one saw you do anything, no one can say you are innocent.

This situation is frightening to Americans, because we have never allowed our society to be ruled by the powers that be. Yet the above scenario is exactly the way that IRS audits occur today. If we discover that the person we elected is not governing in our best interest, we elect someone else. We can't do this with the IRS, and they know this and use this fact to their advantage. There is *no* clause in the IRS tax code that says, "innocent until proven guilty." How do they get away with this?

The answer is not clear, and certainly not reasonable. Some government officials, including some in the IRS, believe that the IRS needs to induce fear in taxpayers in order to ensure tax compliance. Other government officials may think that even though a taxpayer might be innocent, the extra revenue generated from an audit he can't defend means free money for the government. Although it would be political fire to admit to either of these attitudes, former IRS agents and government officials have confirmed these feelings, when they can remain anonymous.

Keep in mind this fact: there is no reason to fear the IRS when, with their notice of audit, they have just told you that they believe you're a liar. There is plenty of reason to be angry.

The IRS allows deductions, and to not take every deduction available to you is like throwing money away. So if the IRS allows deductions, why do they audit you?

The whole reason that audits exist is to force taxpayer compliance. Fear is the best form of control. If someone fears you, they will try to avoid you, and when confronted by you, they will scramble for reasons to get out of your way as quickly as possible. This is the revenue agent's best weapon. He knows that he holds the power in the situation and that you probably fear him, or at the very least you are not as well read in tax law as he is.

It is true that Americans, by-and-large, want to be good Americans. We want to obey the law as much as we can to make life safer. We pay reasonable taxes to make our government strong and capable. When faced with an audit, most of us feel guilty in a way because our government is accusing us of being less-than-model taxpayers. We'd all like to think that we are good citizens of our country.

Recent provisions in the tax code now make it possible to stand on firmer ground when suing the IRS. If you can prove that there was no good reason for them to audit you, and you can demonstrate that you were unduly harassed or abused, then you could have a good case. Unfortunately, even then there is no guarantee that you'll collect on your legal fees.

In June 1997 Mrs. Carole Ward was awarded more than $325,000 in a case that received national attention because of the abusive nature of IRS agents. During a meeting regarding her son's tax return, Mrs. Ward told the IRS revenue agent that she would be better suited for a truck-stop waitress job, with her "big hair" and "clunky jewelry."

The next thing she knew, Mrs. Ward's three clothing stores were shut down by revenue agents, who told patrons that the owners of the store were suspected of illegal drug activity. The agents then discussed her case on the radio and disclosed her tax return information to the newspapers. Mrs. Ward subsequently sued the agency for invasion of privacy—and four years later she won.

Valerie Richardson of the *Washington Times* reported on the progress of Mrs. Ward's case in August 1997, and discovered that the IRS not only has not paid her, but has filed motions to bar the judgment. Mrs. Ward meanwhile is in debt and her legal bills continue to mount. The IRS, with no legal fees to pay, doesn't seem concerned.

In fact, the stories are endless. IRS agents have no incentive to be fair or to side with the taxpayer. Currently, the laws are even stacked toward the IRS. To ensure tax compliance, the government has asked for more jail convictions for tax evasion. While ten years ago more than fifty percent of convicted tax evaders were granted probation, now fewer than thirty percent are not jailed for their actions.

What about Congressional leaders who try to curb IRS abuses? Former IRS historian Shelley Davis writes in her book, *Unbridled Power: Inside the Secret Culture of the IRS,* that, "some elected officials who dared to look too closely at IRS internal operations have found themselves at the other end of an audit, or subject to innuendo, leaks, and other forms of harassment."

If the IRS doesn't have a problem auditing or harassing Congressional leaders who threaten the sanctity of their precious 6103 wall, what harm would it be to use the same tactics with the average American? And who is there to monitor the ethics of these activities? Who is looking over the auditors' bosses?

Forbes magazine reporter Janet Novack interviewed Roger Chastain in March 1997 about his tax conviction. He served four months in a federal prison camp for not paying his taxes. Chastain filed his returns just like other Americans. As a self-employed lawyer, however, he didn't have the money to pay the bills. With penalties and interest, he owed $100,000 in taxes to Uncle Sam.

There are ways to pay your taxes in installments. Form 9465 sent with your tax return tells the IRS that you cannot pay your taxes all at once and would like to set up a payment plan. Be warned, however, that the IRS is not always fair about this option. They tend to intimidate taxpayers who try to use this method to escape paying their taxes all at once. They particularly dislike taxpayers who cannot make their tax payments before the next tax season.

It is perfectly legal and within your rights to pay your taxes in installments. You will need assistance from a prepaid tax service, such as NADN, in order to keep the IRS off your back about paying in installments. Although they would like their money immediately, they would rather receive some money than none at all.

Many people ask what the harm would be in running away from the IRS. After all, in this country it's fairly easy to disappear. In fact, it is estimated that at least two percent of the population is "invisible." What benefits are they enjoying from disappearing from the system?

There are no real benefits from running from the IRS. Some people steal Social Security numbers from deceased or make-believe people, and can go so far as to create a birth certificate and driver's license for a new identity. This crime is a felony; imprisonment is almost certain. Some people have pigeon-holed themselves into cash-only jobs, and while they may earn money tax-free, their ability to receive Social Security benefits, Medicare or unemployment funds is destroyed. Usually, "invisible" people have no access to HMOs, 401-style retirement plans or any kind of insurance. The complete tax freedom of becoming invisible also makes it impossible to enjoy the benefits of paying into the tax system.

Consider these stories of people who have become invisible, or have been invisible and re-entered the tax system, as examples of the potential problems a person thinking about this might face:

* Devin[†] used to be a restaurant owner on the East Coast. He intentionally deceived the IRS on his tax returns for years and claimed fake deductions and losses. When a revenue agent finally notified him of a potential audit, he packed up his things and fled the area. He then proceeded to use the Social Security card of a deceased person to get a job in the resort industry. Although he is successfully invisible in the IRS's eyes, he is also driving with an expired license, he has lost all of his accumulated benefits from his previous jobs, has no insurance and cannot own a home or new car. He knows that he is never completely free and risks being found out one day.

* A woman came to NADN claiming that she had been invisible for years but was absolutely miserable. She was stuck in a cash-only waitress job and wanted to move to a salaried secretarial position in a law firm. She wanted to be a good citizen and begin paying taxes again, but she was afraid of being harassed by revenue agents or even put in jail for her actions. An NADN representative mediated the affair with the IRS and got her on a payment plan so that she could begin earning Social Security and Medicare benefits again, as well as enjoy the peace of mind that comes with doing the right thing.

* Edward Mendlowitz, a CPA and author of *Aggressive Tax Strategies*, includes the story of the former president of RCA Corporation who admitted to the

---

[†] Devin is a pseudonym; this individual is still hiding from the IRS and wishes to remain anonymous.

IRS, after they requested copies of his tax information, that he hadn't filed a 1040 in several years. Although he was fired from his position at RCA and indicted for criminal tax evasion by New York state, the IRS did nothing. Why? He was due refunds every year that he didn't file.

The IRS can and has welcomed back a formerly invisible person. If you are an "invisible" person, it is best to become visible to the IRS again, with the aid of a group such as NADN. When you realize that you need to reenter the taxpaying world, you are inevitably at your most vulnerable because you are in a position to easily be taken advantage of. This is the point at which you need to have a representative who will explain your situation to the IRS and help establish a fair tax payment plan.

Another question some people ask is whether the IRS can track accurate earnings in mostly cash jobs, such as bartending or babysitting. The answer is no. But they try to. Back in the 1970s, the IRS decided that they were going to assess typical earnings for the average bartender, casino dealer, waitress, etc. and closely monitor the tax returns of people in those fields. The IRS even went so far as to have agents hired in such positions so that not only could they get a feel for how much a typical person would make, but find out from other people in the business if cash skimming was a frequent occurrence.

The IRS finally concluded that there was too much leeway in cash-based jobs and constructed an income equation that would determine the average income of most tip- and cash-based jobs. Anyone falling well above or below the average would be subject to audit. While the equation is unknown to most non-agents, countless waiters, bartenders and blackjack dealers can tell stories of harassment by IRS agents.

Even today, the IRS continues to closely monitor tax returns of cash-based occupations. If you are in such a career, monitor your earnings carefully. You must declare your cash earnings as income and, even though cash is not entirely traceable, the IRS already has determined how much you should be declaring each year. *So be careful.*

CHAPTER FOUR

UNFAIR ADVANTAGE

If I have caused just one person to wipe away a tear of laughter, that's my reward. The rest goes to the government.

—Victor Borge

It will be of little avail to the people that the laws be so voluminous that they cannot be read, or so incoherent that they cannot be understood.

—The Federalist Papers

America's beloved folk hero and homespun philosopher, Will Rogers, once made a serious error on his tax return—he overpaid his income tax. Upon realizing his mistake, he notified the proper authorities, explained what he had done, and requested a refund. Then he waited. Waiting didn't seem to work, so he intensified his campaign. Yet, try as he might, he was unable to get his money back from the government. Letter upon letter met with no reply. And no refund.

Finally, he lost his patience, and his typically good sense of humor. In his following year's tax return, Rogers evened the score by listing a special deduction: "Bad debt, U.S. Government—$40,000."

When it comes to the IRS, sense of humor isn't in the lexicon. It seems that money just isn't a laughing matter, especially when it's already in their coffers—or when they think it should be.

Humor has no effect. Letters and plaintive requests can be met with little, if any, response. So how does one go about settling up their affairs with the IRS when there's a dispute? Well, let's start by looking at how they maintain their seemingly impervious, unimpeachable status.

MORE FIREPOWER

The answer to the question, "How long can the IRS hold out?" is another question: "How long have you got?" What citizens and plaintiffs find particularly distressing is that the IRS is able to keep going to court because its legal representation doesn't cost them anything. It costs the taxpayers plenty, but that's not their concern. Winning—or delaying a settlement indefinitely—is. And, in both instances, they do a good job.

Consider the case of Elvis Johnson, a former Galveston, Texas, insurance company executive reported in *Forbes* magazine in 1997. Johnson made a mistake and, in a plea bargain agreement with the IRS, he pleaded guilty to one count of taking an invalid tax deduction of $3,400 on his tax return; for that, he got probation. The more serious problems began when the IRS disclosed the details of this confidential arrangement to the media in 1983, a breach of confidentiality for which Johnson sued the agency.

The case went to trial, and the jury awarded Johnson a judgment of $9 million against the IRS, for their improper disclosure of private tax information. So, naturally, the IRS honored the court decree and paid up, right? Wrong. Fourteen years later, Elvis Johnson, now 75-years-old, is still waiting to see a check from the IRS with his name on it. According to his attorney, Kendall Montgomery, the actual figure with added interest (can't forget that—the IRS never does) is now closer to $16 million.

Johnson is confident that he will prevail in the latest round of appeals. Still, the IRS is holding fast—they show no signs of giving in or settling. In the long run, the agency may emerge the ultimate winner in this drawn-out legal battle by simply outlasting septuagenarian Elvis Johnson.

DESENSITIZING THE AMERICAN PUBLIC

Unfair advantage takes on all kinds of insidious disguises. Having the presence to create media attention can be a major advantage, and the escapades of the IRS lend credence to the adage that there is no such thing as bad publicity.

Daniel Pilla, in his book, *The Naked Truth: Everything You've Always Wanted To Know About The IRS But Couldn't Afford To Ask*, explains this phenomenon.

Each time a particular group of people is attacked by the IRS, and those attacks are published in the national news, Americans become less and less sensitive to IRS attacks. The whole idea becomes more and more acceptable.

He goes on to further underscore areas in which this IRS presence can work against the average American taxpayer.

We have seen that the IRS has designs to create and maintain a sense of 'presence' in the lives of all Americans. We have seen that they have designs to develop a 'taxpayer profile' which will include information they don't need for tax purposes. We have seen that they wish to audit certain businesses even though they aren't suspected of owing taxes.

In other words, you care less and less about what they are doing, and they know more and more about what you are doing.

What can you do about this? If we're talking about the resources and access to technology and media of the average American taxpayer versus the IRS, the answer is not much.

Pilla puts it in perspective when he notes:

The Big Three—organized crime, corporations, and tax shelter investors—can afford to hire the best legal and accounting talent money can buy. But the average American is, by comparative standards, defenseless.

TECHNOLOGY WORKING FOR– & AGAINST–YOU

Not only has technology revolutionized the way the IRS evaluates and cross-checks tax returns and documents, but it has given them yet another advantage over the American taxpayer. With today's electronic tools, computers and software, it's a fair bet that the IRS knows more about American taxpayers in general—and many, personally—than ever before.

Frederick Daily, a tax attorney based in San Francisco, and author of *Stand Up To The IRS*, explains what the new technology means for taxpayers:

> The main difference this year is that there will be fewer correspondence audits; that is, simple questions put to taxpayers through the mail. Part of the reason is electronic. The agency can now better correlate tax documents.

But it isn't just their improved acuity that makes the IRS formidable, it is the disturbing prospect that they now have vast resources for tracking personal spending habits and cross referencing financial records in a variety of complex ways.

"In an audit, the IRS is now looking for everything about you," says Amir Aczel, a statistician at the Bentley College in Waltham, Massachusetts, whose own intense audit compelled him to write his book, *How To Beat The IRS At It's Own Game*.[1]

MIND IF WE COME IN?

"You get an ominous letter: Your tax return has been selected for an audit. The agent asks to meet at your house. Once she's there, she seems curious—about your cars, your kids' school tuition. Suddenly, you realize that she's not just examining your mileage expenses—she's auditing your life," says Mike McNamee in an article in *Business Week*.[1]

"Welcome to the 'financial status audit,' better known as the lifestyle audit. It's the same technique that G-men used in the 1930s to put Al Capone behind bars: Match your living expenses against the income you reported on your 1040. If there's a gap, the Internal Revenue Service may suspect the difference is from off-the-books cash, and its auditors are charged with finding it."[2]

To complete this mission—to find the hidden, unreported cash that, according to the General Accounting Office is estimated to be as high as $62 billion in unpaid taxes annually—the IRS is meticulously training its troops. In 1994, the IRS introduced new audit training programs designed to teach IRS agents how to sniff out those hidden dollars (and tax violations).

"The techniques are nothing new," says Andre Re, national director of the IRS auditing programs. "But many of our agents were rusty or hadn't done this type of audit."[2]

Well, let's just assume they all know how to do it now. And if an audit comes your way, you'll be ahead if you have already checked to make sure that your tax preparer is familiar with the American Institute of Certified Public Accounts guidelines for handling a lifestyle audit. (These guidelines advise tax preparers to ask the IRS to show data that has raised their suspicions, and the nature of the red flags that made them suspect that you were hiding unreported income.) But that measure of protection only goes so far; once again, advantage IRS:

> By statute, the agency must release records gathered in an audit, if requested. However, the IRS does not have to turn over reports from confidential informants.

THERE'S A NEW AUDIT IN TOWN

They're here—the new, improved, super-tough audits, described by those who have experienced them as "audits from hell." The new wave of audits began in 1995, and are being imposed upon selected taxpayers, whose tax returns have been subjected to an unprecedented close, critical, and thorough analysis by the IRS.

"These dreaded line-by-line audits, the first since the late 1980s, make up what is known as the Taxpayer Compliance Measurement Program.

"An audit can cost a taxpayer many thousands of dollars in accounting or legal fees, even if the person ends up owing little or no additional taxes. 'These audits are really an ordeal,' says Bruce Haims of the law firm Debevoius & Plimpton in New York. IRS officials say they need the program to improve taxpayer compliance, gauge how much cheating is going on and figure out how to deter it. They plan to examine individual, corporate, S corporation and partnership returns. Some tax specialists say the audits are so time-consuming that the IRS should reimburse targets for reasonable expenses.

"Forget that idea, the IRS replies."[3]

NO AUDIT, PLEASE SEND CASH

You've gotten past the initial shock of opening a personal letter from the IRS, only to discover they don't want to audit you, they just want you to send more money, now what? If you think they made a mistake, you could very well be right. The IRS makes mistakes all the time.

"Tax experts stress that consumers should not pay anything assessed in error. However, if you get such a notice, check your tax records and respond promptly by calling or, better, writing to the agency. Those who delay are likely to receive far more serious correspondence—actual bills from federal authorities and also from state officials," says Bernard Oster, partner at the West Los Angeles tax firm of Cohen, Primiani & Foster.

"That's because the federal government shares tax information with state governments. If the IRS determines that you failed to report income or claimed unsubstantiated deductions, then that information will eventually reach state tax regulators. And they, too, will send you a bill for additional tax money and penalties." Oster notes that "because state authorities can take longer to assess the tax, your penalties may be greater."[4]

Whatever you do, make sure that before you send any money, you and your tax consultant/preparer, and maybe your attorney, are satisfied that you do in fact owe it. If you ever do send any money in error, you might suffer the same problem as Will Rogers did. And you won't find it amusing that the IRS treats your overpayment like a generous and unacknowledged donation. That's one advantage you don't have to give them—the advantage of owing you money.

REFERENCES:

1. Guy Halverson, "If IRS Knocks, Audit Is Tougher Than Ever," *The Christian Science Monitor*, March 11, 1996.

2. Mike McNamee, "Personal Business: Your Taxes, Audits, Can Your Life Pass Muster?", *Business Week*, February 3, 1997.

3. Tom Herman, "A Special Summary and Forecast of Federal and State Tax Developments," *The Wall Street Journal*, December 28, 1994.

4. Kathy M. Kristof, "More IRS Audits Mean More Tax Questions and More Errors," *Los Angeles Times*, June 26, 1995.

CHAPTER FIVE

THREATS &

INTIMIDATION

Until you heard the titillating tales of IRS abuse from the Senate Finance Committee in 1997, you may have taken with a grain of salt all the horror stories you'd heard about what the IRS does to people. It's true, however, that the IRS has been given almost unlimited power to harass, intimidate, and downright abuse taxpayers into coughing up dollars, oftentimes dollars they don't owe. The agency has the mechanisms, statutes, technology and will to create an environment of fear for taxpayers, and they choose to use their resources. Fear is the impetus that drives most Americans to pay their taxes.

IRS employees have said time and again that they are sent to training programs by their managers to help them master techniques for overcoming resistance from taxpayers who attempt to fight having to pay extra tax money. And it's no secret that stories of taxpayers being forced to give up every luxury they have accumulated in order to pay the IRS routinely hit newsstands near April 15 each year. Perhaps the media solicits these stories, but the IRS certainly has a vested interest in accommodating them, if not proactively initiating the wide circulation of such intimidating stories.

Even accountants fear the power of the IRS; why else would many accountants advise clients to make conservative deductions and not become conspicuous in the eyes of IRS agents? It's in an accountant's best interest to ensure that his or her advice costs little in litigation and time spent defending items on a tax return to the IRS. After all, if an accountant advises you to make a deduction that is questioned by the IRS, this accountant will have to miss work, other clients, and pay for his or her time spent defending that deduction.

And what about the celebrities you hear of who have faced IRS attacks? Common perceptions being what they are, you probably believe that you, too, can easily become a victim of IRS abuse. Willie Nelson, Leona Helmsley and Paula Jones are all good examples of celebrities who have generated much media attention, but also much nervousness on behalf of the average American taxpayer.

According to some IRS critics, however, celebrities receive special treatment from tax collectors because, as Jim McTague reported in a 1996 article that appeared in *Barron's*, the agency is "star-struck."

Sports stars often are targeted by the IRS for not reporting revenue from autograph signings. Some stars choose to use their perks, such as first class flights and free athletic and practice gear, to their benefit by flying coach class and saving the difference from first class or by giving away the athletic wear without having reported such items as income for the benefit of the IRS. Imagine what children who idolize such celebrities think when they see their favorite star in trouble with the IRS. Talk about instilling fear at a young age....

Newspaper mogul William Randolph Hearst subjected himself to an audit when his paper made derogatory remarks about the IRS in 1928. Al Capone, of course, doubled as a mob poster boy, but also as an IRS "Don't Let This Be You" poster boy when he was caught evading his taxes. The IRS achieved a double whammy with this story. Not only did the IRS catch a tax criminal, but it proved itself more effective than the FBI of the so-called "gangster era."

LOSING SLEEP OVER THE IRS

Have you been lying awake for hours around tax season...worrying about what you put on your tax return...doing arithmetical computations over and over wondering if you did everything correctly? If so, you are not alone.

The IRS wants you to feel this way—because they believe it's a great incentive to get you to pay your taxes fully and promptly.

Women have it especially tough with the IRS because of changes when they marry or divorce. Since women change their names, and also are less frequent joint-tax filers, more then three million women every year pay the wrong amount on their tax returns.

Women also have a difficult time with the IRS later in life. Since women tend to live longer than men, they experience problems with the IRS regarding their Social Security amounts and misplaced tax payments. When elderly women receive Social Security benefits from the IRS, they often may not know how much was paid into the fund on their account and, as a result, do not know how much they should be receiving. Recent studies show that the benefit amounts for many women were incorrectly computed and, as a result, are being incorrectly paid—and, consequently, incorrectly taxed.

Remember to look through the benefits that you and/or your spouse have paid to the government. If you find an error, call the Social Security Administration and the IRS to ensure that the problem is corrected.

GEOGRAPHICAL CONSIDERATIONS

Some of you may lose more sleep than others, based on where you live.

Syracuse University has compiled a clearinghouse of IRS information which details IRS activity in every part of the country. One of the items the clearinghouse viewed was audit percentage by location. Las Vegas wins the prize as the most audited city in the country. It is followed close behind by Los Angeles and San Fransisco. Lucky you, though, if you live in Louisville, Kentucky. You are less likely to be audited if you live there than in almost any other big city.

Also, the state of Alaska overall is the most audited state in the country based on audits-per-population. Nevada, not surprisingly, runs a close second. Those of you on the East Coast who thought you would be more suseptible to audits because of your proximity to IRS headquarters actually do not need to worry. You're right around the average in the audit game.

Stories of threats and intimidation by the IRS are not uncommon. It's a sad commentary on the state of our taxation system that this does not surprise us. Recently, we've heard the voices of many citizens who have been victims of IRS abuse. And, while it is clear that some people do evade paying their taxes, they consist of the relative few and should not be the basis for the IRS to presume guilt regarding the rest of us.

CHAPTER SIX

YOU HAVE RECEIVED A NOTICE OF AUDIT

Back in the mid-1980s, a university in the western United States conducted a study to determine the most stressful times in a person's life. The purpose of the study was to reveal what the most stressful incidents in life were, and based on that information, help people confront and control their situations, thus reducing stress.

The two most stress-inducing activities that had a positive outcome were getting married and having a child. The two most stress-inducing activities with a negative outcome were having any kind of communication from the IRS and fear of death.

The astonishing reality for the average person is that the stresses caused by an IRS audit are eclipsed only by experiencing or contemplating death. The recent ballooning of IRS bureaucracy, the focus on individual taxpayers, and the low success rate of audit defenses are indicative of why people fear the IRS.

The National Audit Defense Network's most important mission is to teach taxpayers not to fear the IRS. This chapter will show you what to do when you are audited by the IRS and why you have little reason to fear an audit.

WHEN YOU RECEIVE A NOTICE OF AUDIT

"No matter what the letter says, no matter what the caller asks you, you are under no obligation to respond to any IRS query into your taxes without a counselor or lawyer with you," says former IRS agent Dick Grossman. "In fact, you should hand off your notice to a representative and have him or her handle the situation for you."

When you receive notice from the IRS that you will be audited, they usually ask you to respond within ten days to a certain IRS district office. *Before you call or write the IRS*, contact a group with special IRS expertise, such as the National Audit Defense Network, or your tax preparer, and have a representative handle all IRS affairs, from the first contact you make with them onward. You never know what kinds of questions the IRS will ask you, and it is unlikely that you will know what information they might be fishing for, so the best thing to do is let a professional respond to the IRS on your behalf.

There are several kinds of notices you might receive, and each of them asks different questions.

With the assistance of Dick Grossman, we have compiled below examples of notices the IRS sends.

Although the IRS has been known to call or even arrive in person at individuals' homes or places of business, the most frequent means of communication is by letter. Examples of written IRS communications follow.

EXAMINATION DIVISION NOTICE

A letter from the Examination Division of the IRS informs you that your tax return has been selected for audit. The letter will usually tell you to call a specified phone number within ten days and to produce copies of certain records. The IRS does not necessarily audit all of your tax return; the agent may just look at certain records.

In the mid-1980s a woman who, admittedly, cheated on her taxes sought advice from a former IRS agent, frantically exclaiming that she was being audited and didn't know what to do. The former agent looked at her letter, and immediately told her that she shouldn't worry; her audit was not going to cover the part of her taxes on which she had cheated.

Although in no way do we advocate cheating on your taxes, it is important to know that the IRS does not necessarily scrutinize your entire tax return. Notice carefully what documents you are asked to produce. If you do not have the documents requested, try as best you can to collect as many of your receipts as you can find.

Incidentally, for the last twenty years, according to an anonymous IRS agent, the term "audit" has not appeared on IRS documents. While knowledge-able IRS personnel will tell you that record-keeping is erratic at best, (Shelley Davis, former IRS historian, would be a good person to ask), it is readily apparent that the IRS now describes its audits as "examinations." Hence, the letter from the Examination Division, not the Audit Division. Don't let the terminology fool you; an audit by any other name still elicits fear.

There are two types of audits: a field audit and an office audit. An office audit letter tells you to send in your documentation; this means that you need not see the face of an IRS agent—just send in your information and receive notice of the results by mail. Obviously, if the result of your audit is unfavorable, you may be required to face an agent, but one hopes that will not happen.

It is actually more advantageous for the IRS to perform audits (or "examinations") from their offices, since they save travel and stipend money and the time of an already case-overloaded agent who otherwise must make yet another trip. Since the IRS mission is to collect revenue, however, they will choose the more expensive examination method of visiting you rather than risking the loss of uncollected tax dollars.

Therefore, the field audit exists not only to analyze records in depth but also to put pressure on you. A faceless IRS agent is a lot less intimidating than a person in a business suit showing up at your door with thick hard-bound books full of big words. IRS agents know that you fear this experience second only to the Grim Reaper. The field audit is more intensive than the office audit; the IRS wouldn't spend the extra money for travel expenses if they didn't think there was a financial advantage for them. As a result, it is in your best interest to make sure that you have accurate documentation to show your auditor.

AUTOMATED COLLECTION SERVICE NOTICE

You may receive a notice from the Automated Collection Service. This notice is most often a computer-generated letter that tells you there is a discrepancy between what your tax return says you owe and what you paid. Sometimes this can be a simple adding mistake on your part that you didn't notice, or perhaps the W-2 forms and 1099 forms they have on you do not match your penciled-in earnings. When you receive this notice, the best action to take is to call your accountant or audit defense company and ask them to double check your tax return to ensure that a mistake was made. Then, have them contact the IRS to see what further action needs to be taken. The fees assessed might be worth fighting if they are excessive for the amount of tax owed.

Consider the story of taxpayer Allen Lewis, who made a mistake on his tax return. As reported by syndicated columnist S. J. Diamond in the *Washington Times*, Mr. Lewis received a "Request for Payment" letter from the Automated Collection

Service, which informed him merely that he owed $102.43 in back taxes. Here is the tabulation they provided:

Tax on return	$6,807.95
Total credits	$6,807.94
Underpayment	$.01
Penalty	$102.42
Interest	$0.00
Amount you owe	$102.43

Lewis thought the letter was a joke, and so he ignored it. A month later, another letter arrived, adding 89 cents to the total and threatening to place a lien on Lewis' assets unless he paid up. An IRS spokesperson called the penalty "distorted," but would not go so far as to say that the bill was egregious or even inappropriate.

After discussing the situation with an IRS agent, the matter was cleared, but the fact that the statement was sent in the first place already revealed to Lewis that the behemoth computers at the IRS can blow minor infractions out of proportion.

CRIMINAL INVESTIGATION DIVISION NOTICE

Another type of letter you might receive comes from the Criminal Investigation Division. This is a letter to pay immediate and close attention to. The reason you are receiving this letter is because the IRS thinks you may be evading your taxes. Plan to have your documentation ready and your accountant or audit defense company at your side before you respond to the IRS. When the CID comes calling, you will need a professional representative.

When the IRS does criminal investigations, they sometimes ask neighbors or business associates about your purchasing or investing behavior. Obviously, neighbors or friends do not know the intimate details of your finances, but they can tell an IRS agent about the boat you just bought or your lavish vacation in the French Riviera. IRS agents can determine that your lifestyle does not match your reported income and ask you very detailed questions about where you've been spending your money—so be prepared to have good explanations for everything.

You might also be a source for someone else who is being audited by the IRS. Agents may come to your door to ask you questions about someone you know. Keep in mind that you never have to say anything you feel uncomfortable saying, and you can tell agents that you have no comment for them. NEVER LIE.

Until the past few decades, members of organized crime or drug lords were the most sought after targets of CID investigations. Although they continue to be CID targets, the IRS has expanded its investigations to include private citizens who may be involved in money laundering or other questionable activity. Anyone whom the IRS thinks is hiding income from them is a potential target.

Al Capone will live in infamy not necessarily because he was a famous gangster who eluded the authorities on several occasions, but because he was caught by the IRS for evading his taxes. Auditing has become one of the biggest tax compliance tools in the agency, but *it is important to remember that you never have to give up your rights when you are being audited.*

CHAPTER SEVEN

EVEN ACCOUNTANTS TREMBLE

Government, even in its best state, is but a necessary evil; in its worst state, an intolerable one.

—Thomas Paine

When men get in the habit of helping themselves to the property of others, they cannot easily be cured of it.

—U.S. Supreme Court
Flora v. United States

If your tax preparer doesn't want to sign your tax return, does that mean he or she is worried that they may not have done a thorough and accurate job? Not at all. What it means is that tax preparers can make mistakes and, consequently, they are at risk for penalties. Some of those penalties may be imposed by the same agency that may penalize you, and they can face the same deleterious consequences: fines, loss of business (temporary or permanent), and mountains of red tape, legal expenses, and wasted time.

But accountants and tax preparers also have to answer to their clients. Sometimes, acting in good faith, they can make mistakes that cost their clients money, and in turn, the clients will sue them to collect that money, as well as more for damages.

HOW DID ALL THIS START?

Prior to 1976, the tax preparer who signed an income tax return held no liability for it. Very few Internal Revenue code provisions affected the conduct of persons who prepared income tax returns for a fee. The Tax Reform Act of 1976 changed all that, and had a direct effect on tax preparers—and taxpayers; it was as part of this legislation that the Tax Preparer Liability Act of 1976 was passed. At first, it was regarded simply as a nuisance; to many tax preparers, it appeared to be an insult to their integrity, a joke. But as time went on, the joke became no laughing matter. As this Act was strengthened—and enforced—it bred widespread confusion and, in some cases, fear among tax preparers, CPAs, and even tax attorneys. Why? Because the IRS had the power to enforce the new rules by imposing penalties and seeking injunctions.

Basically, the Tax Reform Act of 1976 adopted rules to regulate, through disclosure requirements and ethical standards, the conduct of income tax return preparers; that is, persons who prepare income tax returns for others (including claims for refunds), in exchange for compensation. What's more, the person does not have to be the only preparer or the signature preparer of a tax return to qualify under the tax preparer liability provisions— the Act says that anyone who helps in a substantial portion of the preparation of a tax return (in exchange for compensation) can be liable for these penalties.

As a result, people unrelated to the actual preparation of the return (such as real estate brokers, stockbrokers, financial planners, and others who give advice related to the tax consequences of an individual's return) have been assessed penalties by the Internal Revenue Service for erroneous advice they may have given.

WHAT ARE THE ACTUAL RISKS AND PENALTIES?

PREPARER PENALTIES

The following table, compiled by former IRS agent Pat Cavanaugh, indicates the penalties that can be applied against a tax practitioner.

IRC Section Penalty	Applied Violation	Against Employer	Against Employee	Amount of Penalty
Identification Penalties				
6695(a)	Failure to furnish copy of return to client	Yes	No	$25.00 per failure
6695(b)	Failure of preparer to sign return	No	Yes	$25.00 per failure
6695(c)	Failure to furnish identifying number	Yes	No	$25.00 per failure
6695(d)	Failure to retain copy of list of returns prepared or to maintain a listing of clients	Yes	No	$50.00 per failure (not to exceed $25,000 per person per return period)
6695(e)(1)	Failure to file employee return or keep list of preparers and returns they prepared	Yes	No	$100.00 per failure

6695(e)(2)	Failure to provide all information required on reports required by 6695(e)(1)	Yes	No	$5.00 per item (penalties imposed by 6695(e)(1) and (2) not to exceed $20,000)

Conduct Penalties

6695(f)	Endorsing or negotiating a tax refund check	Yes	Yes	$500.00 per item
6694(a)	Negligent or intentional disregard of rules and regulations	Possibly	Yes	$100.00 per return
6694(b)	Willful understatement of liability	Possibly	Yes	$500.00 per return
6701	Civil Aiding & Abetting	Yes	Yes	$1,000 per individual, $10,000 per corporation per return
7206	Felony false statements & aiding or abetting	Yes	Yes	$100,000 per individual, $500,000 per corporation, 3 years imprisonment or both
7207	False list, ID # or other fraudulent document	Yes	Yes	$10,000 per individual, $50,000 per corporation, 1 year imprisonment or both

[b] The conduct penalties are the ones about which practitioners worry most, especially the $100.00 Section 6694(a) penalty for negligent or intentional disregard of rules and regulations. This was described by one of my graduate students who is an IRS Revenue agent as the fiscal equivalent of a speeding ticket.

Practitioners should be very concerned about getting these speeding tickets because if you get too many (only Leslie Shapiro, the Director of Practice knows just how many is too many) you can be made a part of the IRS Practitioner Project under which a larger part or all of the returns your firm prepares can be audited.

Ii] My experience and the experience of others (*see BROCKHOUSE V. U.S.,749F.2d 1248 (12/13/84), ssAFTR2d85-44s*) is that the use of Data Questionnaires (Client Organizers) and Office Review Procedures are the most important factors in guarding against a practitioner penalty.

[ii] See also Rev. Ru1.80-265 and Rev. Ru1.80-266 as well as Rev. Proc.80-40 for the importance of Data Questionnaires and Office Review Procedures.

The following case studies present examples of some of the consequences incurred by tax preparers who have signed their clients' tax returns.

CARELESS RESEARCH RESULTS IN CIVIL DAMAGE AWARD AGAINST ACCOUNTANT

In one case, a client consulted his accountant about the proposed sale of property owned by the client. The accountant advised the client that it was his understanding that the sale would not be subject to federal or state income tax.

The client sold the property and, based on the advice he had received, he did not report the gain. Later, when the Internal Revenue Service performed an audit, the client was assessed additional taxes for the gain on the sale of the property. In the course of the audit, it had been determined that the sale was in fact a taxable incident—not a nontaxable one, as advised by the accountant.

The client, having acted upon the advice of his accountant, blamed the accountant for the error, and took legal action. The result? The CPA has a settlement to his malpractice insurance carrier of more than $35,000.

INFLATING DEDUCTIONS RESULTS IN CONVICTIONS

The law states that preparing a return which is fraudulent or false, or committing perjury in preparing a return, is a felony punishable by a fine of up to $5,000 or imprisonment of up to three years, or both, plus liability for the costs of prosecuting the case.

One CPA found that out the hard way. He was convicted on five counts of aiding and assisting in the preparation of false or fraudulent income tax returns, and was sentenced in Federal District Court to serve prison terms of two years for each count.

What did he do to earn this conviction? Basically, he put things down on the tax returns that couldn't be backed up by the records. He understated gross receipts by $10,000, and listed various deductions in excess of what the records justified; in another return he deducted a number of items without basis in the records. He incorrectly prepared a corporate income tax return by including a deduction of $317,000 for accrued purchases that were not justified by the corporation's records. He also overstated purchases by $15,000 and $42,000 respectively in two other corporate returns without basis in the records.

Was he trying to cheat for his clients? Maybe, maybe not. He could have been acting on information given to him that he didn't take the time to substantiate. The fact is, if he signs his name on the tax form, it is assumed that he has done all the fact-checking necessary to satisfy himself that what he is recording for the IRS is accurate and complete. Ignorance—of the facts or of the law—is no excuse.

In another case, during a routine audit it was discovered that at least one deduction listed as an expense had not been incurred and had not even been submitted as an expense to the preparer.

The preparer contended that the erroneous deductions were the result of inadvertence rather than intent to commit a crime. The IRS argues that the preparer's motive was to have satisfied customers who came back to him year after year because they received a refund. Who won? Not the preparer—he was convicted of a felony.

IGNORANCE, NEGLIGENCE—SAME THING

In one case, the negligence penalty was imposed because the preparer deducted a Subchapter S Loss in excess of the shareholder's basis in the stock—a violation of Code Section 1374(c). The preparer admitted that he was "not familiar" with this Code Section when he prepared the return, but the court affirmed the imposition of a $100 negligence penalty and concluded that the resulting underpayment of tax was due to the preparer's "disregard of the express limitation of Code Section 1374(c)."

Conduct penalties, such as the one just described, are those about which the tax practitioners worry most—especially the $100, regarding Section 6694(a) penalty for negligent or intentional disregard of rules and regulations. This has been described as the fiscal equivalent of a speeding ticket.

Practitioners are very concerned about getting these speeding tickets, because if they get too many (and only the IRS Director of Practice knows just how many is too many), they can be made a part of the IRS Practitioner Project under which a larger portion or even all of the returns their firm prepares can be audited.[1]

Not Planning to Pay the Penalty? Watch Out...

An attorney who prepared tax returns was faced with a penalty for failure to write his Social Security number on the returns he prepared. The attorney disagreed with the penalty and chose not to pay it. No problem, the IRS just levied against his bank account, taking what they needed to satisfy the score, and called it even.

And the hits just keep on coming.

If the Tax Reform Act of 1976 seemed to create confusion and difficulty, it pales in comparison to the newest tax reform measure—the Tax Reform Act of 1997. Tax experts are more in demand than ever, as taxpayers and tax preparers alike try to wade through the ever-burgeoning quagmire of new rules, regulations, and penalties. The addition of new penalties and the expansion of old ones to such levels as $500,000 fines and five-to-ten years in prison, as well as the removal of the right to prepare tax returns as a professional, all have substantially undermined the ability of tax preparers everywhere to properly help their clients determine the best tax reduction/avoidance methods to be used.

The problems created by the mere possibility that the IRS can impose these penalties has cost preparers countless hours and dollars defending themselves on positions adverse to the IRS, and also make these preparers' liability provisions more punitive than was the likely original intent.

A tax preparer now has to be a detective—he or she cannot ignore the implications of information received from you or of which they have other knowledge. When information as furnished appears to be incorrect or incomplete, the preparer must make reasonable further inquiries. In one case, in which the tax preparer was found liable for the negligence penalty, the IRS held that there was lack of due diligence where a preparer claimed the same deduction in one year that was disallowed on an audit in the prior year. Although the preparer was aware of the prior year audit, he had failed to follow through with the audit results.

HOW FAR DOES THE LIABILITY EXTEND?

One IRS district is trying a case in which the preparers of returns are being held responsible for the information provided to them on any partnership K-1 form. The preparer's responsibility applies, even though he or she may have had nothing to do with the preparations of the partnership return itself.

In this test case, the preparers are expected to verify the information on the K-1, and could be held liable for negligence under the due diligence regulation if they do not verify that proper accounting procedures were used. They are further responsible for the accuracy of asset evaluation, for the proper structuring of financial instruments, and for correct procedures of tax filing, including the depreciation method selected.

And hold on, new changes are on the way. "The IRS officials said they would seek to expand their ability to evaluate data on partnerships and partners as they modernize the agency's computer systems through the year 2001. They said they would test the feasibility of matching information documents with partnership returns and encourage partnerships to file their Schedule K-1 electronically so that it is easier to match them with their partners' individual returns."[2]

THE FIVE-HUNDRED-DOLLAR PENALTY

For each return in which a preparer willfully attempts to understate tax, a $500 penalty will be assessed. If a tax preparer disregards any information provided by a client, and that results in an underpayment of tax, then he or she may be subject to this penalty, even though the IRS states that the preparer's client is the one ultimately or primarily responsible for the accuracy of his or her own return. Why? Because the preparer is still expected to make reasonable efforts to insure the accuracy of the return.

For example, if a client makes unusually high deductions, such as charitable contributions, the preparer should ask for an explanation of that figure because it should raise a red flag. If the preparer fails to inquire further, it may result in the assessment of penalties against the preparer. The same scenario applies to interest or other expenses that might seem excessive, as well as to miscellaneous deductions.

What then if, in later years, the understatement of tax is eliminated by a net operating loss carryback? That might let the taxpayer off the hook, but not the preparer—he or she may still be subject to the willfulness penalty.

A $500 penalty also will be assessed against any preparer who endorses, executes, or in any way handles another person's income tax refund check—even if they have been directed to and given permission to do so by the client. This penalty will be assessed whether or not there is reasonable cause and also whether or not the preparer was acting in a legal capacity with a power of attorney.

PENALTIES FOR EVERYONE

Not only do penalties get increasingly harsh in terms of dollars, but when you consider the fact that they can be assessed in the form of unlimited numbers of concurrent penalties relating to the same return, there is no wonder that there's plenty of trembling going on.

Civil penalties of $1,000 and up can be imposed for knowingly aiding and abetting an understatement of tax liability. If the understatement is on a corporate return, the penalty is $10,000. And, of course, the aiding and abetting penalty also may be imposed in addition to other penalties that may apply. What's more, everyone can get in on the act—the penalty can be applied to any person who aids or assists with any portion of a return or other document, knowing that it will be used in conjunction with matters that arise under the Internal Revenue laws and also knowing that an understatement of another person's tax would result. This penalty applies regardless of whether the taxpayer had knowledge of or gave consent to the understatement. While the $100 negligence and $500 willfulness penalties apply only to income tax preparers, the penalty for aiding and abetting an understatement of tax liability applies even to those who do not charge for their services.

PRISON IS NOT MERELY A THREAT

As if they weren't already intimidated enough by the threat of excessive fines, tax preparers have another nightmare to contend with—doing time. The penalty for improper disclosure, meaning the unlawful use or disclosure by a tax preparer of information obtained in the preparation of a tax return, is a misdemeanor punishable by fine, imprisonment, or both. In fact, the punishment can be imposed whether or not the disclosure was intentional.

But the real attention-getter is the felony charge—we're talking some serious money and hard time. A preparer who willfully aids or assists in the preparation of a tax return or refund claim, which is false or fraudulent as to any material matter, is guilty of a felony. If convicted, the fines can run as high as $100,000, imprisonment of up to three years, or both, in addition to the cost of prosecuting the case. In the case of corporations, the fine is $500,000, with the same opportunities to go to prison and foot the bill for the prosecution.

In one case, an indictment under this section was sustained even though there was no under-statement of tax. In this particular case, the preparer completed a client's gift tax return, falsely reflecting that the client had made certain cash gifts to the preparer and members of his family, apparently trying to get a tax advantage for the client. Any time a preparer understates income or overstates deductions, he or she may be found guilty of aiding or assisting in the preparation of false or fraudulent returns. This, of course, is a felony offense, and will be discussed in detail in the following chapter.

REFERENCES

1. *Your Income Taxes: A Special Report* Why Your Tax Preparer Doesn't Want to Sign Your Return

2. David Skidmore, "Auditors Criticize IRS Efforts To Police Partnerships," *The Associated Press*, June 21, 1995.

CHAPTER EIGHT

TAX FRAUD IS A SERIOUS MATTER

The tax laws reflect a continuing struggle among contending interests for the privilege of paying the least.

—Louis Eisenstein
The Ideologies of Taxation

"Potius sero quam numquam."
(Better late than never.)

—Titus Livius 59 B.C.—A.D. 17

ATTENTION, PLEASE

When the IRS audits taxpayers, they can initiate criminal investigations for tax fraud if they feel there are grounds for such violations. If the investigation turns in the direction of tax fraud, this is a very serious matter. If you or anyone you know is in this situation—get help immediately! Retain the best legal representation you can afford, and do it now.

DEFINING FRAUD

It is not illegal to plan your financial holdings in a manner to keep your taxes as minimal as possible—it's smart business. It's your right to minimize and reduce your tax obligation; in fact, many people overpay their taxes every year (to the tune of billions of dollars), simply because they (or their tax preparer) are unaware of the laws and codes that apply, or because they fail to exercise their options in taking advantage of the deductions that are available to them. Taking full advantage of the rights, protections, and opportunities available to you is not a crime. Tax fraud, however, which means to use deception to illegally reduce your tax obligation, is a very serious offense.

Tax fraud includes the filing of false records, documents, statements, and returns. It also sometimes involves conspiracy to defraud, attempted tax evasion, abetting or counseling fraud, and willful failure to file tax returns.

According to the Internal Revenue Code, Section 7201:

> Any person who willfully attempts in any manner to evade or defeat any tax imposed by this title of the payment thereof shall, in addition to other penalties provided by the law, be guilty of a felony and, upon conviction thereof, shall be fined not more than $100,000 ($500,000 in the case of a corporation), or imprisoned not more than five years, or both, together with the cost of prosecution.

Code Section 6653(b) provides for civil fraud penalties as follows:

If any part of an underpayment of tax required to be shown on a return is due to fraud, there shall be added to the tax, an amount equal to 50 percent of the underpayment.

And, of course, since penalties can be stacked, it is possible that a taxpayer could have both criminal and civil penalties levied against them for the same offense.

In order to establish a charge of willful fraud, the IRS must prove the following: that the taxpayer committed the act with intent, knowledge, and purpose. It is key that all three of the conditions exist at the time the tax return was prepared or, in a failure to file situation, when the return was not filed. To be found guilty of willfulness, the taxpayer must have been aware of the result of his or her act.

"You must believe that the omission of income or the gross deductibility of the item in questions will result in an illegal understatement of your tax liability," says former IRS officer, Jack Warren Wade, Jr. "You must intend to commit the act in question and your purpose must be to understate your tax liability. There must also be a definite understatement of tax liability. The fraud penalty is an actual percentage of the deficiency or the tax unreported. If there is no tax, there can be no penalty."[1]

HOW DO THEY DO IT?

To understand how to protect yourself from committing a fraud offense, you need to understand how the IRS carries out a criminal tax fraud investigation.

Each District IRS Office has a Criminal Investigation Division, whose main mission is to carry out criminal tax fraud investigations within that particular district. There are IRS special agents assigned to the Criminal Division who are trained and experienced in undertaking such investigations. At times, these investigations use the assistance and cooperation of regular IRS agents and other law enforcement agencies. To conduct intensive in-depth investigations, the IRS sometimes organizes special "fraud squads," or "strike forces."

What's more, the IRS Criminal Division can also use other law enforcement resources, such as the U.S. Department of Justice, local offices of the U.S. Attorney, and state and/or city District Attorney offices. If a cannon with that sort of firepower is aimed at a taxpayer, that's a staggering arsenal against which to attempt a defense. In addition to knowing who are the adversaries, being familiar with the process and procedure of a tax fraud case is critical to designing a successful defense of the taxpayer.

HOW DOES A TAX FRAUD CASE GET STARTED?

Tax fraud cases can be initiated in a variety of ways: "squeal" letters, informer tips, or unusual circumstances that bring a taxpayer to the attention and scrutiny of the IRS. In some cases, an IRS special strike force may be carrying out a wide-ranging probe of suspected criminal activity, or targeting a particular group of taxpayers or a individual taxpayer.

If you are ever approached by a Special Agent of the IRS, on the initial contact he or she must inform you that they are a Special Agent and give you the IRS warning and statements about self-incrimination and other stipulations.

If the case is criminal in nature (for example, receiving income from unlawful activity, or concealing income), a regular IRS agent cannot be used as a ploy to hide the true intent of the investigation as a criminal tax fraud investigation, or to obtain statements, information, or other evidence that normally would require a search warrant.

> If a Special Agent gives the proper identification and warnings, the taxpayer or his or her representative can politely refuse to answer any questions or give any information, and immediately consult experienced tax counsel about the case. On the other hand, if the Special Agent fails to give the proper identification and warnings, any statements or evidence illegally obtained by the Special Agent before his identification and purpose were discovered, may be suppressed in an action brought in the District Court.[2]

HANG ON TO YOUR CONSTITUTIONAL RIGHTS

If the IRS Special Agent is playing by the rules by properly identifying himself or herself, and gives the taxpayer all the warnings and disclosures, and the taxpayer still cooperates and willingly makes statements and disclosures, then that information provided by the taxpayer can and will be used in a criminal proceeding against the taxpayer. Federal court cases have verified that the taxpayer, in such an instance, has waived any Constitutional rights against the use of statements or evidence used to find him or her guilty of federal tax violations.

If you find yourself being interviewed by an IRS Special Agent, it would be wise to shut up immediately. It is in your best interest to tell the agent politely that you will be speaking to and retaining legal counsel to represent you, and that your attorney will be contacting their office. Be polite and brief. Remember, anything you say can be used against you.

Many well-meaning citizens keep talking and talking, trying to appeal to the agent and to explain their innocence. Potentially, a big mistake. Do not jeopardize your situation further by resorting to any kind of an explanation. Realize that the agent is gathering information; they are either recording you on tape or making mental notes which they will promptly transfer to written notes as soon as the encounter with you ends. To a naive and uninformed taxpayer, what they may innocently and inadvertently utter might be a crucial statement that ultimately helps put them behind bars.

WHEN SIMMER TURNS TO FRY

One of the most difficult situations is when, in the course of conducting a routine civil examination, an IRS agent discovers evidence of fraud and turns the case over to the Criminal Division. In this instance, neither the taxpayer nor his or her representative is informed of the shift from a regular examination to a possible criminal tax fraud case. Therefore, little can be done except to attempt to suppress the use of evidence and statements given in the regular examination as evidence in a criminal tax fraud case.

TELLTALE SIGNS THAT SIGNAL A TAX FRAUD INVESTIGATION IS UNDERWAY

1. The IRS agent suddenly requests all deposit slips, bank statements, canceled checks, bank books, brokerage statements, and other investment statements to verify all items on the return.

2. The IRS agent begins making copies of numerous items, especially names and addresses of customers and suppliers.

3. The IRS agent asks for written statements of net worth, use of monies, or cost-of-living expenditures.

4. The IRS agent asks for permission to search through the taxpayer's files, or his or her accountant's or tax preparer's files.

5. Employers, customers, suppliers, banks, brokers, or other persons notify the taxpayer that they have been contacted by the IRS with regard to their dealings with the taxpayer.

6. The IRS agent, after doing many of the aforementioned things, advises the taxpayer that he has to suspend his examination at this time due to other pressing matters, such as temporary reassignment to another case (or to attend a series of meetings, or to take over another agent's casework due to an illness, promotion, whatever), but promises to contact the taxpayer again in the near future.

In circumstances like these, especially if the agent suddenly suspends the examination, the taxpayer or his or her representative should ask the agent, preferably in writing, the specific reasons for suspending the examination, and further, they should inquire whether the agent has made any recommendation or referral of the case to the Criminal Division or any other IRS office. This step is crucial, because if a referral has been made to the Criminal Division and the agent admits it, appropriate measures can be taken to demand a return of all statements, information, and evidence given to the agent so they cannot be used in the criminal investigation. Of course the demand would probably be refused and would require that a proceeding be brought in the District Court to attempt to suppress such evidence, but at least the taxpayer would be aware of the situation and have his or her legal representatives working on the case from the beginning.[3]

SECRET TAX FRAUD INVESTIGATIONS

Sometimes the IRS Criminal Division will conceal their investigation of a potential criminal tax fraud case. An unknowing taxpayer could be deceived or misled about the real intent of the investigation if the Special Agent does not properly identify himself or herself and give the proper IRS disclosures and warnings.

Be wary of the IRS agent's questions and intentions if any of the following actions or patterns occur in the course of a routine examination or process:

1. Two IRS agents (without identifying themselves as Special Agents, or giving any IRS warnings or statements of rights) come to the taxpayer's home, possibly in the evening, and are very friendly and apologetic, but ask questions about the taxpayer's finances and family situation.

2. An IRS agent calls the taxpayer and invites him or her to the IRS office to discuss their tax returns, and asks the taxpayer to bring all deposit slips, canceled checks, and all other financial information as mentioned previously.

3. The taxpayer receives an IRS letter or a call from an IRS agent expressing the desire to examine his or her tax returns, and the place of the examination is in a District Office different from the taxpayer's own home District Office. (For example, where a taxpayer living on Long Island, New York, who would normally be examined at the Mineola Branch District Office, receives a letter or call from the IRS requesting the taxpayer to come to a District Office located in New York, New York.)

4. During the course of an examination by an IRS agent from another District Office (as in the above item), the taxpayer receives an IRS letter or a call from an IRS agent from his or her home District Office that the same tax return has been received for examination.

5. The taxpayer receives an IRS letter or call from an IRS agent to examine his or her tax return for a year on which the normal twenty-month examination cycle has expired, such as a request in October 1997 to examine a 1994 tax return.

6. Employers, customers, suppliers, banks, brokers, or other persons notify the taxpayer that they have been contacted by the IRS about dealings with the taxpayer.

More recently, the IRS has begin many "sting" operations, where Special Agents posing as prospective buyers of businesses which do a large cash business, try to get admissions of concealment or skimming of cash income by the present owners as part of the negotiations for a higher purchase price than income per books would support.[4]

So What Happens to Taxpayers Who Get Convicted?

The news is full of dramatic examples of what happens to people who are unlucky enough to be prosecuted by the federal government for tax fraud. The penalties are harsh, even extreme. Here are some examples of recent cases that have gained the attention of the media; in case they failed to grab your attention the first time around, or may not have been publicized in your area, read on.

Council Woman Convicted of Tax Fraud Sentenced to Thirty-Three Months in Prison

Former Councilwoman Patricia Moore was sentenced Monday to thirty-three months in federal prison for extortion and income tax fraud, despite her lawyer's repeated assertions that her constituents needed her back.

Moore, who rose to local and even national prominence as a fiery critic of Los Angeles police abuses and a commentator on the 1992 riots, stood silently as U.S. District Judge Consuelo B. Marshall announced her decision.[5]

Moore was also sentenced to twenty-four months supervised release, 2,000 hours of community service, and had to pay a fine of $700 for her convictions on two counts of failure to file income tax returns and thirteen counts of extortion. At the time of sentencing, Moore indicated that she planned to appeal her case and asserted that she was set up by FBI agents who were out to frame black politicians. She claimed she was tricked into accepting a bribe from a government informant who pretended to be a business executive seeking to do business with the City Council. Moore said that the informant became her lover and induced her to accept a payoff of $50,100 from Compton Energy Systems, which was seeking Council approval to build a waste-to-energy conversion plant, as well as a payoff of $12,334 from Compton Entertainment, which needed Council permission to open a card casino.

MARTIAL ARTS SCHOOL FOUNDER GETS FIVE YEARS FOR CONSPIRACY TO SKIM CASH PROFITS

John C. Kim, the founder of a national chain of martial arts schools who was convicted of tax fraud in federal court last December, was sentenced Thursday to five years in federal prison.

Kim, formerly of Naperville, was involved in a conspiracy to skim millions of dollars in cash profits and evade income taxes on the money.[6]

Federal District Court Judge James Holderman, before sentencing the martial arts school owner, stated that Kim was "the undisputed organizer and leader" of the conspiracy to skim cash profits and to evade the payment of income tax. Judge Holderman said, "It wouldn't have taken place without (Kim's) acquiescence and approval and willful participation."

INDIANA HAIR CARE PRODUCTS COMPANY OWNER PLEADS GUILTY TO TAX FRAUD CHARGES

The owner of an Indiana hair-care products company pleaded guilty Thursday to two counts of filing false tax returns for 1989 and 1990.

Ernest Daurham, Jr., 50, of Olympia Fields admitted he understated his income and claimed personal expenses as business expenditures. He faces up to three years in prison or fines of $250,000 on each count or both, according to the U.S. Attorney's Office of northern Indiana.[7]

The hair care products executive, who owns D-Orum Hair Products Inc., in Gary, Indiana, which manufactures Leisure Curl and other personal care products, also owns and operates a chain of beauty salons in northwest Indiana and the Chicago area.

The case first came to light when Daurham was charged by city officials for using his home for business purposes. Apparently, the businessman had been renting his estate to others for fees of up to $10,000 for four hours. The incident kicked off an ever-deepening investigation into his extensive business operations. The IRS got involved and uncovered his understating of income as well as his claims for business-related expenses, which were actually personal expenses.

TWO BROTHERS WHO OWN SIZZLER RESTAURANTS INDICTED; FACE UP TO 115 YEARS IN FEDERAL PRISON

Two successful brothers who co-owned a chain of Sizzler restaurants in New Jersey and New York were accused of cheating the company and the IRS by skimming cash profits of almost $1 million dollars.

Indictments of tax fraud, mail fraud, and conspiracy charges were filed against the two men, Sewdutt "Mike" Harpaul of Hauppauge, New York and Chandradutt "Ronnie" Harpaul of Woodmere, New York, according to Frank Nixon, IRS District Director.

The brothers face up to five years imprisonment for each count of each charge against them, or a total of 115 years. They could also be fined up to $100,000 each for tax evasion and fined up to $250,000 for each mail fraud and conspiracy charge.

According to the indictment, the brothers had the Howell store manager set aside receipts from each day's lunch for them to pick up, and that income was not reported on their business or individual federal income tax returns. The Harpauls underreported their gross receipts by the same amount in monthly invoices sent to Sizzler, which required them to pay a royalty fee based on a percentage of the gross receipts, Nixon said. The brothers kept a second set of books that tracked the skimmed cash.[8]

FORMER COUNTY PROSECUTOR'S HOME IS AUCTIONED OFF; WIDOW BEGINS SERVING TWENTY-SEVEN MONTH PRISON SENTENCE

The Somerset Valley Bank foreclosed on the home of the former Somerset Country Prosecutor who committed suicide in a Nevada casino in November 1996, while awaiting sentencing on federal charges of tax fraud and embezzlement.

> The former Prosecutor, Nicholas L. Bissell Jr., was under house arrest and was facing as many as ten years in prison after being convicted on federal charges of embezzlement, tax fraud, and abuse of power. He had cut off the electronic monitoring bracelet he was required to wear and fled two days before he was to be sentenced. He shot himself inside a hotel room in Laughlin, Nevada.[9]

The late prosecutor's widow, Barbara Bissell was also convicted on tax evasion and theft charges, and began serving a twenty-seven month prison term at a federal institution in Danbury, Connecticut.

NON-PROFIT CHILDREN'S CHARITY CHARGED WITH FRAUD; YEAR-LONG INVESTIGATION BY FEDERAL, STATE AND LOCAL AUTHORITIES

Even nonprofit foundations and charities are not immune to federal tax investigations and charges. The Jewish Education Center, a group that raises money to assist seriously ill children by urging people to donate their own cars to the charity, has been charged by the government with fraud, diversion of funds, and false advertising following a year-long investigation by federal, state, and local authorities. (The charity ranks among the top fifty for-profit used-car chains nationwide. In 1996, the

Jewish Education Center had sales of $8.5 million.) In this case, a charge of civil fraud attracted the attention of the IRS, who undoubtedly smelled smoke and thought fire.

> The San Francisco District Attorney's office charged the nonprofit organization with civil fraud and false advertising...while the state accused it of violating charitable trust laws. The IRS is investigating for possible tax fraud and money laundering. The government agencies also won a court order to seize the center's assets. The Center couldn't be reached for comment.[10]

WELFARE QUEEN PLEADS GUILTY TO TAX FRAUD; HER SON AND HIS FIANCEE ALSO FACE UP TO TEN YEARS
(This one from the Some-People-Never-Learn Department.)

> Fourteen years after she was convicted of what may still be the largest welfare fraud in history, a Pasadena woman pleaded guilty Monday to new felony charges of defrauding the government of $89,000 by submitting bogus tax refunds.

> Dorothy Mae Woods, 55, who in 1983 was dubbed a 'welfare queen' for collecting $377,500 in welfare as a dozen different people while living in a mansion, pleaded guilty to conspiracy to defraud the government, U.S. Attorney Nora M. Manella said.[11]

Woods' son, Leonard Bernard Palmer, 38, and his fiancee, Clarissa Lanell Anderson, 36, were charged with aiding and abetting the making of false tax claims; they pleaded guilty to forging about 160 federal tax returns using the names and Social Security numbers of low-income people. According to the federal prosecutor, each of the three faces up to ten years in federal prison.

FORMER CHIEF FINANCIAL OFFICER OF BAY AREA JEWEL FIRM INDICTED ON TAX FRAUD CHARGES

Federal prosecutors have indicted the former chief financial officer of a San Francisco jewel firm on federal tax and fraud charges. Former Golden ADA business executive Ashot Shagirian, 41, was indicted by a federal grand jury on charges of tax evasion, filing a false tax return, and conspiracy to defraud the government.

> The 41-year-old Shagirian, who formerly resided in San Francisco and Largo, Florida was arrested in San Juan, Puerto Rico, on April 11 (1997) by the U.S. Marshal's Service and U.S. Customs Service with an assist from Interpol.
>
> According to the indictment, Shagirian sold his Golden ADA stock in 1994 for $2.5 million and then falsely claimed that he lost $1.1 million in real estate dealings in Armenia. Prosecutors said that Shagirian, who authorities said fled the United States in 1996, engaged in this scheme by getting Armenian citizens to make fake purchases and sales agreements.[12]

Shagirian, if he is convicted, faces up to thirteen years in prison and a fine amounting to $750,000.

WHAT DOES THIS MEAN TO THE AVERAGE TAXPAYER?

Well, you might not be dealing with such huge sums of money as have been described in the previous articles, but you should be aware that the penalties don't take into account how much money you are dealing with when it comes to tax fraud. Sure, the fines might not be as stiff, but the prison sentences are an equal-opportunity adventure for the rich and poor alike.

It may be inferred from some of the examples that there are certain groups, ethnic or otherwise, who may be the targets of extra-close scrutiny and in-depth investigations. A claim like this could hardly be substantiated, and we don't intend to make it; what you infer is your own business.

REFERENCES

1. Audit-Proofing Your Return, Jack Warren Wade, Jr., Macmillan Publishing Company, (*year*), p.238.

2. Emil Sebetic (former IRS trial attorney with the IRS Regional Counsel's Office at New York City and Adjunct Associate Professor at Fordham University Law School), *The IRS Practice Guidebook*, (Richard Gallen & Company), p. 96-97.

3. Emil Sebetic, p. 100-101

4. Emil Sebetic, p. 101-102.

5. Jeff Leeds, "Moore Gets Sentence of 33 Months," *Los Angeles Times*, May 13, 1997

6. "Martial Arts School Founder Gets 5 Years in Tax Fraud" *Chicago Tribune*, July 25, 1997

7. T. Shawn Taylor, "Businessman Pleads Guilty to Tax Fraud" *Chicago Tribune*, April 4, 1997

8. "Brothers Indicted for Fraud Scheme at Sizzler Restaurants," *Dow Jones News Service*, April 10, 1997

9. Somini Sengupta, "Prosecutor's Home Auctioned," *The New York Times*, August 11, 1997

10. "Charity Charged in False Advertising Probe," *The Wall Street Journal*, June 16, 1997

11. "Woman Pleads Guilty to New Tax Fraud Charge," *Los Angeles Times*, July 8, 1997

12. "Jewel Firm Executive Indicted on Tax Charges," *The San Francisco Chronicle*, April 23, 1997

CHAPTER NINE

PREPARATION IS THE BEST DEFENSE

Good fortune is what happens when opportunity meets with preparation.

—Thomas Edison

AND NOW, THE GOOD NEWS

By now, you are probably well-acquainted with the other news. And, if you've been with us thus far, you have read example after example of what not to do—and how you can get into trouble by doing nothing at all. Now it's time for a lesson in action: How to put yourself in the best possible position to avoid an audit, or in the event that you are unlucky enough to have one come your way, how you can come through it virtually unscathed.

In her book on personal finance, Linda Chandler, a national authority on entrepreneurial leadership, capital formation, and values training, and former Senior Vice President of Sutro & Co., wrote:

> For the majority of Americans, the largest total dollar expenditure made in a lifetime will be for federal, state, and

local taxes. Of these, the largest and most pervasive, no matter what the state of residence, is the federal tax burden.

The good news is that we are still, by and large, left to determine the amount of our annual taxes on our own. We can still institute strategies that effectively reduce and sometimes eliminate burdensome taxes. This is the best news there is regarding income tax.

For the average American, learning how to become tax-savvy is one of the biggest annoyances a person will face, but the experience can also be quite rewarding. As one hears repeatedly throughout life, "knowledge is power." Knowing what kinds of things IRS agents will look for, knowing how you can best prepare your audit defense, and carefully reviewing any materials you either receive or send to the IRS will give you tremendous power in the taxation game.

You should not wait until you receive the notice of audit to set in motion your tax defense. The IRS tax code changes almost every year, and since your financial situation, your bills, and your assets also change every year, you need to brush up on current tax issues. For example, in 1997 alone Congress created educational incentives for children, new capital gains rules, and new income phase-outs for many provisions.

Countless financial advisors recommend that to have your best defense, you must have a good offense. Therefore, you must stay abreast of tax code changes and make sure your financial adviser also knows about them. Don't assume that your adviser will know about all tax changes; you may find that he or she is not aware of the particular tax changes that benefit you. Also, you will need to know what tax changes you can take because your accountant or adviser may know about tax deductions, but may not want to take any that are risky.

WHAT'S YOUR FAIR SHARE?

Maybe you're thinking that it will be difficult to sort out which of your expenditures may become tax deductions. You may even feel intimidated at the prospect of searching for effective tax advantages that will work for you. Some people even feel like they are being unpatriotic by trying to pay less in taxes, and they may sincerely desire to support social programs that make use of tax dollars.

Everyone has these feelings. It is important to remember that you *are* paying your fair share to the government when you pay your taxes. There is a fine line, however, between paying your fair share and paying more than your fair share.

Americans for Tax Reform, an organization in Washington D.C. that specializes in tax issues, holds a "tax-free day" every year that celebrates the day in the year when people have stopped spending their paychecks on the government and begin spending them on themselves. The day is now in July. So, if you begin paying your taxes on January 1, you can start spending money on yourself around Independence Day. Does this make you feel better?

We are not advocating not paying taxes. It is true, as the engraved quote on the IRS building states, that "taxes are what we pay for civilized society." If the government ran more efficiently, and if people pay their "fair share" of taxes, our government should run a surplus. Pay your "fair share," but not a penny more.

Also, remember that the IRS has a different definition of "fair" from yours. The IRS definition of "fair" means to find every penny that you could *conceivably* owe and charge you for it. Your definition obviously is to pay what you *definitely* owe. So use the proper definition; after all, you are the only person who will look out for you.

How to Prepare for a Meeting with Your Tax Preparer

What does your tax preparer normally do when you meet? Does he or she take the information you provide, ask a few questions, and then do his or her best to fill in the boxes appropriately? Does he or she ever try to prod your memory a little on areas you may have overlooked? How about making suggestions for changes you can make in the future that will help reduce your tax liability?

As with any service provider, there is a quite a range of possible service. A preparer who merely takes your information and fills in the blanks is, in fact, doing his or her job, but not necessarily rendering you the level of service that will help you make the most of your money. On the other hand, a tax preparer who goes beyond what is expected at the basic level, and tries to help ensure that you are taking every deduction allowed to you is an asset. And a tax preparer who gives you advice that you can use to help reduce your future liability is a treasure.

How can you get the best possible service from your tax preparer? In the first place, you need to be prepared. You should have a good idea of what your total income is, and by estimating your deductions in advance, you can come up with an anticipated gross income figure. At this point, you will already have in mind a rough estimate of the taxes you will owe. Having this knowledge at hand when you go into the meeting will give you confidence—you'll feel in control of the situation. The better prepared you are at this point, the more you stand to gain.

Because you will already have a pretty clear idea of what your tax liability will be and are prepared, the amount of work required by the tax preparer will be reduced. This will help keep the hourly fees down. An added benefit of being well-organized and prepared is that the accountant or tax preparer will not be burdened with trying to get the basic information from you, and she will be able to concentrate on helping you do some fine tuning. She will be more inclined to apply her expertise to helping you find deductions that you may have overlooked, things that a professional might be aware of that you may not. This is your opportunity to utilize her talents and knowledge for those areas where you may require guidance.

What's more, because you have your records in order, and documentation that has given you the ability to be so well-prepared, you will not feel intimidated or fear an audit if one comes your way.

Always keep your objectives in mind when meeting with your tax preparer. After all, you are the customer, and you have the right to expect the tax preparer to do her best work for you. That's what you pay her to do, isn't it?

A CONFLICT OF INTEREST?

It's important to remember that accountants and tax preparers may act as much in their own interest as they do on your behalf. They have certain obligations to consider when they sign your return. As we have seen, they can be subject not only to penalties imposed by the IRS, but to legal action being taken by their clients as well; it's s only natural that they will be inclined to protect themselves. If you feel there is any sort of conflict between you and your tax preparer, sort it out between yourselves, and do it right away. You don't want to get into an audit situation and have to deal with it at that time.

What sorts of things might come up that would pose a conflict between a client and a tax preparer? In the case of an audit situation, it may be possible that your accountant has previously encountered the particular auditor you have drawn. If this happens, it is vital that you understand any preexisting relationships or predilections before your turn comes up for review. If your accountant or tax preparer has any hesitancies about representing you, find out before you go for the audit. You need to know just what kind of support you can count on from her, and you need to know that no conflicts will surface between you during the audit—a potentially costly predicament in more ways than one.

One more thing: Be sure to determine where you fit within the scheme of your accountant's business. Do she have the time and interest to fulfill the commitments you require of them? Does she give you the feeling that your work is important? Is she willing to go to bat for you in the case of an audit? And, if so, are you confident of her work and her ability to support what she has done for you? These are important questions that you need to resolve in your mind in order for you to have a good working relationship with any accountant or tax preparer. And, should an audit ever arise, you need to be confident that you are working with the right person.

WHAT ROLE DOES THE ACCOUNTANT OR TAX PREPARER PLAY IN AN AUDIT?

In the event of an audit, you are going to need all the help you can get. Naturally, you want the active involvement of your accountant or tax preparer as your representative. In this role, one of the things you can expect is that she will put a stop to any extraordinary hassle you may be experiencing as a result of repeated audits. An accountant can also move the review up to the supervisory level when necessary. An accountant can also agree to extensions of time, although you will probably want her to agree only to limited extensions whenever the statutory limit draws near.

Whatever you do, don't go to an audit alone. If your preparer suggests that you go alone, find out why. Even though you may believe you are well-prepared, the circumstances of meeting an auditor face-to-face can be disconcerting, to say the least. If she is unwilling to go with you, bring another representative, even a lawyer if you can afford one. Then find a new accountant.

DON'T TRY TO REPRESENT YOURSELF IN AN AUDIT

When—If—the time ever comes to face an audit, you are going to need some help. An audit can be confusing, intimidating and overwhelming. If nothing else, you'll appreciate the reassurance of having someone there with you, even if you feel that you are thoroughly prepared. And if there is ever a dispute over what transpired, or if at some point you may need to request that some evidence be suppressed, you will have a built-in witness already in place—and someone to back you up.

"Most people in unfamiliar territory in which they experience high levels of stress tend to overreact," says Linda Chandler. "This reaction may take many forms, but...almost needless to say...none of these forms are particularly positive. Your objective is to get the results you can for yourself. You want the best representation to accomplish this. If you think it is *you*...think hard before proceeding!"

It's important that you not let feelings of frustration, desperation, anger, or despondence overwhelm you. Know that they are normal, and then do your best not to let them stand in your way.

AN AUDIT IS A REVIEW OF YOUR DOCUMENTATION

Basically, an audit is nothing more or less than an impartial review of the deductions you have taken and the documentation you have to support them. (You do have documentation, don't you?) *Always remember that documentation is key—you must have it.*

You can look at it this way: you have your objectives and the IRS auditors have their objectives. IRS staff are not policemen (although you may feel just as intimidated as if you were stopped for speeding), they are people trying to do their job, which is to collect money. Your money. They are actually more like detectives on a mission to make sure that you can justify what is on your tax return. On the other hand, you have a mission of your own: to emerge from the meeting without being required to give them any more money or, perhaps, to get some money back.

Even though you have been assured that your return was selected at random, chances are there was something that triggered the audit; even so, it may not be obvious to you (or even to the auditor).

What you are there to provide is backup (your documentation). If you do provide anything new or additional, just be sure that it is in your own best interest. You are required be honest, and to provide material on the issues directly in question. Never provide any extraneous material, or offer information on areas of your return that are not being directly questioned. It's best to be polite, but there's no sense in overdoing it. IRS auditors are not known for their sense of humor, so don't try to be cute—it's not going to make them sympathetic, and it will probably just annoy them.

Important guidelines for your audit, as reported by numerous financial advisers, are:

1. Never let go of your original documents!!

2. You are the only one who will be held responsible for having the documents, so hold on to the originals.

3. Take copies for your tax preparer, accountant, and the auditor...but...*no originals.*

GET IT RIGHT FROM THE BEGINNING

Preparation is your best—and only—defense in the ongoing battle over your tax dollars. And part of preparation is learning about the legitimate and legal means that will allow you to shift expenses from the nondeductible category into the deductible column. The best way to do this is to examine your ordinary expenses—the major categories being shelter, food, transportation, entertainment, and health. See if you are overlooking anything that could help you make your dollars go further.

In order to make your tax dollars return to work for you, you need to stay informed—keep up to date on all the changes that directly and indirectly affect you. Shelter strategies will come and go; tax laws change constantly. You'll need help, too, from good advisers who can help you keep more of what you earn.

"If you can approach your relationship with the IRS as a contest of wills and knowledge, you will hone your ability to come out on top more often," states Chandler. "The 'Tax Game' is a major component of the 'Money Game.' So the better you learn to play the first, the better you will do in the long run."[1]

REFERENCES

1. Linda Chandler, *It's Just a K.I.S.S. Away: A Woman's Guide To Winning The Money Game*, Learning 200 Press, 1994.

CHAPTER TEN

DOCUMENTATION & RECORDS

WHO PREPARES THE RETURN

Probably the best recommendation that could be offered in terms of tax return preparation is this: *Don't prepare your own tax return.* As the years have passed and Congresses have come and gone, nuances and complexities have been gradually added to our tax code and now it is impossible to navigate effectively without a tour guide. So, if your tax return is any more complex than a simple arithmetical computation (and most people's aren't so simple), you will need the advice and assistance of a licensed tax professional.

Licensed tax professionals are attorneys who specialize in tax law: certified public accountants (CPAs), public accountants (PAs) and/or enrolled agents. There are also other types of preparers who are bonded by various government agencies, such as those allowed by the State of California's

Registered Preparer Act. Following are descriptions of all such tax advisers and what kind of specialized help they may offer you.

TAX ATTORNEYS

Attorneys who specialize in tax law may be the best overall preparers as far as determining how your situation would be interpreted, given the facts and circumstances of your case. They are, however, very expensive and spend a great deal of time reviewing documents that you have prepared for them, rather than doing the documentation itself.

CERTIFIED PUBLIC ACCOUNTANTS

Certified Public Accountants and Public Accountants are essentially the same designation as far as tax law is concerned. The CPA is a professional title granted an individual so that he or she may audit for Securities and Exchange Commission purposes and financial institution purposes for various financial statements, primarily prepared by businesses and corporations.

Public Accountants are people who have met certain educational and experience requirements and, due to the longevity of their practice, are given this designation. In both cases, as far as tax law is concerned, CPAs and PAs may or may not have a background in specific tax law, although many do take continuing education classes related to tax issues. They will help you in the documentation and record-keeping necessary if there is an audit by a government agency on the particular tax return, but they may be a little weak in the legal interpretation of the various code sections. They may or may not be expensive, depending upon the area in which you live and the extent to which they rely upon tax preparation for their livelihood.

Enrolled Agents

Enrolled agent is a special designation granted to an individual by the Internal Revenue Service. There are two ways to become an enrolled agent: one is to have five years of experience at a level of competency within the Internal Revenue Service that requires the regular application and interpretation of Internal Revenue Code.

The second way is to pass a test administered twice annually. In either case, a moral and ethical practice background investigation of each individual applying also is required in order to attain enrolled agent status. This is used to determine whether an applicant has followed certain guidelines in the filing and preparation of his or her own individual tax returns. Also, there is now a requirement that each enrolled agent must complete certain continuing education units to maintain his or her professional performance and competency.

Other Types of Tax Preparers

There are a number of other types of preparers available to individuals who have met certain requirements of training. H & R Block tax preparers is one such example. People who work for institutions such as H & R Block usually attend a course or school which gives them basic background instruction related to individual income tax law. In some states, such as California, there is a registration procedure in case of consumer complaints related to their preparation of an individual return. While there is a requirement for the registered preparer to acquire continuing education units each year, including related updates in income tax law, there is not any regulatory background investigation of these individuals related to their professional or educational knowledge.

Another method of obtaining help outside of a paid professional is to find a local Voluntary Income Tax Assistance organization (VITA) that helps in the preparation of individual returns for lower-income W-2 wage earners and senior citizens, in addition to other people in the community if they have the ability. VITAs are usually run by local colleges in conjunction with IRS instructors and utilize university-level accounting students to help in the tax return preparation and advice.

Finally, you can always use the buddy system when filing your tax return, but only if the returns are easy enough for a novice tax preparer to analyze. An in-law or other relative, if you are comfortable with someone like this being privy to your financial information, can help you remember those tax deductible purchases you made and can also tell you what they did on their return. When you look at your helper's return in this buddy system, you may find a deduction that you could have taken! In general, the more pairs of eyes that do the arithmetic and research the deductions, the more audit-proof your return can truly become.

In general, whether you pick a licenced professional or a regular tax preparer who may be unlicensed, it is important to utilize a professional since he or she has a better chance of being aware of certain changes in the law that may require forms of which you are unaware. You may have a better understanding of the tax law and how it applies to your situation, but an omission of certain forms can create problems for you even though there is no tax consequence to these forms.

IF YOU DECIDE TO PREPARE YOUR OWN TAX RETURNS

If, however, after care considering the option of professional return preparation, you still decide to tackle the job yourself, here are some guidelines that will assist your brave quest. Remember, tax professionals will help you, sometimes for very reasonable fees.

FAMILIARIZE YOURSELF WITH THE TAX LAW AS IT APPLIES TO YOU

Whether you decide to obtain the help of a tax professional or to do the tax return yourself, there are certain things you should be aware of. *Regardless of who prepares the tax return, you, as the individual filing the return, are fully liable for all entries made on the tax return.*

Therefore, it is in your best interest to keep yourself fully aware of the basics related to tax law and how it applies to your financial life. If you do your tax return yourself, there are a number of things you can do to help yourself. You can choose, as many people do, to take a tax course, much like those a professional tax preparer might take through a professional educational network—or try your local university or community college. Such a course is geared to helping people understand income tax laws and will help you understand your tax situation, if you are not yet aware of where you fall within the tax structure.

If you do not have the time to attend a series of classes, you may find it helpful to review the various publications made available by the IRS through the Government Printing Office. The two most common and general publications available are Publication 17, related to your individual income tax, and Publication 334, for small business tax preparation. Both cover items—in certain instances on a line-by-line basis—that you would find on an individual tax return.

Publications 17 and 334 are available at most IRS offices that have a walk-in Taxpayer Service Division. Also, at these departments are a number of the more commonly used specific publications related to items such as payroll taxes, travel and entertainment, auto use, etc. You may also obtain copies of the general publications or specific pubications by calling the 800 number in your area for taxpayer service and ordering these through this alternative. You may also write directly to the

Government Printing Office and obtain a list of all the publications related to IRS topics that it has available on its list.

All the publications issued by the IRS are helpful in identifying general terms related to any specific issues on an income tax return. It should be remembered, however, that these publications are merely narrative interpretations of the law itself, and as such are not binding upon the IRS if they do, in fact, conflict with the law as written initially.

It is also worth noting that these publications are usually printed on an annual basis and therefore do not reflect the week-to-week changes that may occur in any specific law as a result of revenue procedures or Congressional interventions that change the tax law. Sometimes, Congress can change the tax law retroactively, so combing your newspaper for tax changes can be financially rewarding.

The key to using IRS publications or their toll-free and walk-in services is to remember that the person you deal with or the manual you read is an extension of an immense, behemoth bureaucracy. You may get information that will help you and, to the IRS's credit, it has helped many taxpayers find answers to questions. *Remember to write down and document every person you talk and what advice they give you.* Oftentimes, you will have one person tell you that something is fine, then someone else tell you that it is not. Accurate recordkeeping of your correspondence with the IRS will minimize such behavior. Consequences of bad advice are detailed below.

THE IRS IS NOT BOUND BY ITS OWN ADVICE

Although you may have received advice from an IRS agent to do one thing, the agency is not officially bound by their own bad advice. A paper trail will help your case if you are questioned on bad information, but don't expect complaisance from the IRS if your argument is at all weak.

Consult with a professional tax consultant, one who has dealt with the IRS before, to find out if your advice from the IRS was valid. Two minds in agreement will help ensure accuracy.

KEEPING ACCURATE RECORDS IS A GREAT AUDIT DEFENSE WEAPON

The Internal Revenue Code, specifically Code Section 6001, mandates that every taxpayer have certain records as required by the IRS.

In turn, IRS regulations require that any person required to file an income tax return must keep 'such permanent books of account or records, including inventories, as are sufficient to establish the amount of gross income, deductions, credits or other matters required to be shown by such person in any return.'

Also, Code Section 7203 stipulates that as a taxpayer, it is unlawful to keep any records and not declare them on your tax return. It is in your best interest as well to keep such records in an easily accessible location.

Why keep good records? Countless accountants, IRS agents or attorneys will tell you that keeping good records means that you can establish your case, spend less time worrying about where to find things and will establish early credibility with your auditor. After all, someone who has to fish for a document will not look very organized, and could have easily made up the deduction.

Because people tend to remember things as they do them, or immediately after, organize your files as you get them, and file them in labeled, orderly folders. You can call a folder, "W-2," another "home office expenditures," etc. The more specific your folder, the easier it will be for you to find a particular item. Some home business people use separate folders for office supplies, monthly utility paperwork, and the like, and this helps to further separate their expenses into neat categories.

Another method you can use to keep your records is to go through your bank statements, indentify all checks and debits relating to various personal and business expenditures, and record what you bought and why, and how much you spent.

Then your bank statements, which list your checks in numerical order, will be an organized in a space-effective way of remembering your finances. Any person questioning your finances need only look at the statement to know when you bought the office furniture or computer.

The final word on record-keeping is that you can never be too cautious when keeping records. Every little detail is not too much to handle when you face punishment for making unallowed deductions.

CHAPTER ELEVEN

STRATEGIES FOR WINNING YOUR AUDIT

The IRS has a system for determining whether you will be audited, and it's important to know exactly what that system is for a successful audit outcome.

There are a few major characteristics that IRS agents look for when they decide which tax returns to audit. Here are the main red flags that will make your tax return stand out:

DEDUCTIONS THAT EXCEED IRS DEDUCTION LIMITS

You might itemize your deduction and accidentally do the wrong math, or you may make an exceptionally high deduction claim for a particular item. In either case, you have become a red blip on the audit screen. If you have made the mistake due to math, then you will receive the obligatory "miscalculation letter" from the IRS. If you have taken an extraordinarily large deduction that you did make, keep every piece of related documentation so that you can show any questioning agent your actual purchase and have the deduction allowed.

ARITHMETICAL MISCALCULATIONS

Anytime you make a math mistake, your tax return becomes more noticeable. You will receive a letter telling you that you have made a math mistake, and they will expect you to pay whatever difference you might owe in taxes—with penalties, of course. This mistake is a common one, and unfortunately it triggers audits if it is grievous, or if another suspect item comes into focus after the initial math mistake is noted.

DOCUMENTATION THAT ARRIVED BEFORE YOUR TAX RETURN

Your W-2 and interest reports from banks and lenders had better match your tax return or you will receive the letter. Another common mistake that taxpayers make is to assume that banks do not send copies of such materials, or to assume that the IRS does not pay attention to them. For both theories, don't bank on it. The IRS, if it thinks it will make money, will absolutely check everything they have. It's the other aspects of their tax operation that tend to be suspect.

LIVING ABOVE OR BELOW YOUR MEANS

The IRS definitely pays attention to where you live and what kind of job you have. Earlier, we mentioned that there are certain equations the IRS uses to determine your audit ratio. Well, the IRS also knows where you live and will not believe you if you decide to claim poverty, even though you have a hot-shot job on Wall Street, drive a German sportscar and live in a spacious colonial in Connecticut.

Watch these red flags; you will make yourself almost audit proof if you attempt to make your tax return as inconspicuous as possible.

Another mental note to make is that you theoretically could be an IRS auditor, so think about the kinds of things you would probably look for in a suspect tax return. Are your deductions not jiving with your receipts? Are you claiming awfully low income for a thriving business? Are your rental property losses legitimate looking? Note such items and you will be as good as the eyes at the IRS that will also look at your return.

Higher income brackets are more subject to audits than lower income brackets, not only because higher income people claim more deductions but also because they are statistically more likely to pay their IRS debts, whether owed or not. The worst "crime," then, is that people who have extra income might spend it frivolously on the IRS, when they really don't owe any money.

You have no power when you are under audit regarding time, location and what documentation is requested of you. You must show up at an IRS designated time and place and provide whatever papers are needed. Although agents are supposed to choose places and times convenient to the taxpayer, do not assume that this will happen.

If you choose to drag on the proceedings, no one will stop you. The IRS has been known to drag on cases themselves for many years, and since they are paid by taxes, they have nothing to lose. You, however, could postpone and delay hearings but you will pay for them in one way or another. If you are found guilty during your audit you will be slapped with additional penalties, and if you are found innocent, you will still have paid the extra time for whatever representation you have chosen. It is best to proceed according to the IRS timetable.

In fact, the general rule to follow is to be as flexible as possible until your rights or abilities are infringed upon. Your chances of winning an audit really depend on all the factors we have mentioned previously:

Are your documents is order? Do you have explanations for every item the IRS wants to know about? Are you hiding anything? You must turn the tables in your audit and put the IRS on the defensive for auditing you in the first place. If you can honestly say that all your documentation matches your deductions, you are confident in your deductions, and you can have your tax professional back you up on your claims, you will rarely lose.

Taxpayers do have rights in audit situations. If you do not like your ruling, appeal. If you have been treated unfairly, tell someone and even bring legal action if you can. Congress has recently granted more rights to taxpayers when fighting the IRS in audit situations. Use your increased rights. Fight the IRS and you might be pleased with your outcome. Although the IRS plays dirty, you now have Congress on your side.

Chapter Twelve

Tax Advantages
For Businesses

Owning a small business or working out of your home presents excellent advantages for you, but also incessant headaches from the IRS. The freedom and satisfaction of working for yourself is the fruit of your determination to make your business succeed. For home-based business owners, your lack of a commute creates a much more productive work day. However, your bubble of self-satisfaction faces a steel spike every April 15.

So you think you've made it impossible for the IRS to find fault with your business activities? Well, you say, you document every purchase your business makes. You write down every client you see, you photocopy and file every check that leaves the office, and you meticulously review and file all of your associate employees' tax information as well as your own. You think you've covered all your bases, right?

Not so fast. The IRS has a way of finding the innocent glitch, the forgotten oversight, or a vague section of your tax return and blowing it into a case of intentional tax deception. Your innocuous 1040 given such loving care by you has become an embarrassing blemish that you actually feel guilty about, even though you know you did nothing wrong.

Wouldn't it be nice to receive notification that you are being audited, and be able to rest easy, knowing that every deduction you've taken and every penny you've saved was within your rights as an American taxpayer? So many people overpay their taxes because of the dreaded audit that hard-earned money is literally being thrown away to the tax-collecting bureaucracy. The IRS does not donate extra tax revenue to the poor or needy, as you might with extra income; the IRS feeds the bureaucracy.

With the proper tools, you can maximize your income and minimize your debt to Uncle Sam, while being perfectly within your rights and 100 percent legal. The tools you need—tax strategies, a professional tax adviser assessing you if necessary, and detailed documentation—will save you thousands of dollars on your taxes. With the amount of taxes small business and home business owners pay, it's about time all available deductions are taken. If the IRS wants to audit you, you can open the door and let them plow through everything; you are confident and worry-free because you've paid your taxes already.

Read these strategies for saving thousands of dollars through legal tax deductions for your business. If you do not have a home business, create one. If you already have a home business, make sure you are taking every deduction available to you.

OWN A HOME OFFICE

The best tax-saving business in town is right in your own home. You can deduct thousands of dollars in taxes by owning a home business. And really, a business based in the home is the most flexible, easy to manage and non-confining you can find.

The first thing you will need to do when planning your home-based business is to decide where you will put it. IRS regulations stipulate that you must have a portion of the house dedicated to this business and nothing else. Therefore, you must find a room that you can devote exclusively to the needs of your office. Then, you must document that you have this room. Take a picture of your home office and/or draw a diagram of your home's dimensions, sectioning off the office space. If you happen to have a blue print of the home, marking off the office space on the document would also suffice.

You need to be able to prove that you use your home office only for business activities. Keeping a journal of the clients who came to see you and what phone calls you took at the office helps show that you have made the room an official office. Until recently, the IRS generally ruled that you must actually see clients and hold business meetings in your office to qualify for a home office deduction. However, a recent provision allows you to use your office for managerial and administrative activities, provided you have no other location to conduct them. In other words, be prudent with your home office and treat it as an office and nothing else.

When you create your home business, you will need people, including the IRS, to know who you are and what services you offer. Purchase letterhead, business cards, and invoices with your home address printed on them. Not only will this inevitably add credibility to your business as a whole, you legitimize the business in the eyes of a suspecting party, such as a revenue collector.

You can deduct the portion of the mortgage that covers your home office on your taxes every year. For example, if your office takes up ten percent of your home's square footage, and you pay $1,000 a month on your mortgage, you can deduct $1,200 a year from your taxes.

Common areas of your home are also tax deductible if clients use them. For example, the hallway between your office and the front door, the bathroom next to the office, and the wet bar that houses coffee and sodas across the hall qualify as tax deductions. This amount of square footage can constitute 25 percent of your home's mortgage. As an example, assume that right now you're deducting $3,000 a year from your mortgage payments.

You can take these deductions even further. Do you own a company car? Most home business owners also have to visit clients, so a company car is probably necessary. You can deduct the portion of your mortgage that covers the square footage of the garage where the car is parked. So now you are utilizing 30 percent of your home's space for your business. You're saving more than $3,500 a year.

Obviously, the startup costs associated with your business are tax deductible. If you double your home phone as a business phone you cannot deduct the expenses, but you can if you create a separate phone line. Your first phone line in the home, regardless of use, cannot be deducted from your taxes. Your office furniture, your electronic equipment and the portion of your utilities dedicated to the office can all be deducted. You've just saved yourself several thousand dollars!

Now that you're ready for business, you'll need some employees.

Hire Your Children Tax-Free

Your children ages 7-18 can provide you with additional tax savings. When you hire them to work for you, their wages are tax-free, up to $4,000 annually.

Your fledgling home business might need a bookkeeper, or an administrative assistant to handle incoming phone calls and type your correspondence. Or maybe you need a weekly office cleaner to empty the trash, vacuum and dust. What better employee than one you can pay tax-free!

The stipulations regarding the hiring of your children include paying them a reasonable rate. Minimum wage, obviously, is the least amount of money you can offer them. You also must log the hours they worked and what job they performed. You must also submit proper W-2 and 1099 forms on their behalf at the end of the year.

By hiring your children to work for you, you create not only a tax incentive but also a way to teach your children the value of money. They can help pay for their clothes, their school supplies and their Friday night entertainment.

This tax tip is available to you regardless of whether you own a home-based business, but you can certainly utilize it while building your home business.

JOB PROSPECTS IN MAUI (OR NEW YORK, LAS VEGAS OR VAIL)

You provide an excellent business service that you need to market. Also, your home business needs some new clients. It's time to take a trip.

Traveling greatly reduces your personal expenses, but it is costly for a business but there are several ways you can increase your travel deductions. Some creative planning and meticulous documentation are all you need to travel for business and pleasure—and cheaply at that.

Your husband has taken a week off from his job to prospect for clients with you in Maui. You believe that there are businesses in Maui that would greatly benefit from your services, and you certainly need a secretary to help you with organizing your materials and taking notes. Your husband can become your employee, and as long as there are valid business prospects in Maui, you can enjoy both meeting with clients and meeting the waves!

If you decide to travel by car, there is no limit to the number of people that can travel with you. Your wife can travel with you and any business expenses you incur are tax deductible. A romantic dinner for two will not survive the deduction chopping block, but a dinner with your wife and a potential client is acceptable.

If you're driving a long way, consider that the IRS believes that 300 miles of driving in one day is a full day of business travel. Your business trip could be planned around this number. If you are on the way from Seattle to Los Angeles, or maybe from New York to Atlanta, plan to drive 300 miles and stop somewhere fun or historic and have a great time. Note, however, that you must continue to drive in the same direction as your final destination at all times for the trip to be tax deductible. Stopping in San Francisco might be all right on the way from Seattle to Los Angeles, but Reno is not a justifiable stopover.

A final note to all of these travel strategies is that you must spend fifty percent of your trip, including travel days, on business. If you can document at least half of your time to client meetings, presentations and the like, you can deduct the entire trip. As with all deductions, however, be prudent with your spending and realize that you cannot justify extravagant personal purchases.

Become A Corporation

The innumerable tax savings available to you when you incorporate are too profitable to not partake of.

Any individual can incorporate. A sole proprietorship or a partnership can be incorporated. There is a huge tax incentive to do so. A section of the Internal Revenue Code allows for the tax-free startup of a corporation. The only stipulation is that if you owned the company before incorporating, you must still own eighty percent of the company after incorporating.

To become a corporation, you first need to contact an organization, usually called a "corporate headquarters," which will incorporate you in a particular state. Many people who want to start a corporation do so in Nevada because that state has a "hands off" policy toward corporations. A single person can be a corporation. You can be the entire Board of Directors and Officers. You can make corporation purchases, hold stockholder meetings, draw up a company mission, and go to business meetings—all under the blanket of being a corporation.

Gifts For Your Clients

When you treat your clients to special perks, you must be wary of how you do it. If you want to claim the maximum tax deductions, you must keep the following information in mind.

Generally, when it comes to meals and entertainment, you can only deduct fifty percent of the cost of your activities. For example, you can take a business associate to lunch and discuss business, but you still must pay taxes for half the meal. You can only deduct half the expense for taking a client to a baseball game also.

Your travel expenses, however, are fully tax deductible. You can take a taxi ride to the business lunch and deduct the entire trip. Also, if you had to spend the night at a hotel after the baseball game, you can deduct 100 percent of the cost. Your hotel room is a travel-related expense.

A requirement for claiming a tax deduction is that you must discuss business during your activity. If you have a business dinner but never mention the business, you are not eligible for a tax deduction. How do you prove that you discussed business? Well, the IRS must take your word for it, but any documentation you might have that shows that you discussed business; such as a note pad with ideas written on it, a business card or brochure from your client, or a presentation folder from the evening, will certainly not harm your credibility.

Currently, you do not need any sort of documentation for business meals under $75. You can document that they took place and what was discussed and claim your fifty percent deduction. For meal expenses of more than $75, a receipt and more detailed presentation information will be needed.

Note that these requirements apply to all kinds of entertainment activities. You can discuss business on the putting green and deduct half of your cart rental, food, beverages and greens fees. You can also take your clients to a Broadway show and deduct half the cost of the tickets, but you cannot *give* your clients tickets to a show, without going with them and discussing business, and expect to claim any deductions.

OTHER BUSINESS TAX INFORMATION YOU MAY NOT KNOW

It's not surprising that there are several documented cases of people who thought they were doing the right thing, but who ended up being mauled by the IRS steamroller when they turned in their 1040s. Who can blame these poor souls? There are countless shades of gray in the IRS tax code when it comes to deductions you may or may not take while you are at work or conducting business activities.

Consider these stories that have become case studies in the ambiguity in the IRS tax code:

* A woman generated extra income for herself as an organist for weddings and special events and deducted her business expenses from her tax return. When the IRS contacted her about her return, the agent asked her if she enjoyed playing the organ. She said, "Oh yes, I really do enjoy playing the organ; in fact I've been playing since I was a child." The agent responded by telling her the deductions would be

disallowed because she played the organ as a hobby, and it did not qualify as a legitimate business.

* A grocery store employee was told that he had to stay on the premises at all times during the work day in case of emergency. Therefore, during his meal breaks he purchased products from the store, ate on the premises, and then deducted the costs of his meals as a business expense. The IRS did not allow his deductions, claiming he could have brought his meals from home.

* A business owner paid more than $160,000 in kickbacks to secure business for his trucking firm. He deducted this amount from his taxes. *His deduction was allowed in full.* Because his payments were not illegal under state or federal law, and because his company needed the business, the business owner's claim was approved.

Although you may think it's easy to dissect the thought process behind the walls of 1111 Constitution Avenue, think again. No matter what your expertise is in going to bat against the IRS, you can never be prepared for the curve balls.

CHAPTER THIRTEEN

TAX ADVANTAGES FOR RETIREES

For most people the word "retirement" conjures up two simultaneous images. One image is of the white-haired couple tooling around the interstate in a Winnebago. The other image is of a frail elderly woman counting pennies to afford a basic necessity. With the two images in mind, most Americans invest in their retirements so as not to have to face financial hardship.

Ironically, for all the talk about retirement poverty, seniors are among the wealthiest Americans. Today's seniors are by and large products of the Depression; they know what happens when there is no money and they believe that risky investments are at best unreliable. Today's seniors have been frugal with their major purchases and have invested fairly conservatively. With maturing IRAs, wise investments, savvy saving and a with a little help from Social Security, today's seniors are financially much better off than many generations of seniors before. *The IRS knows this.*

The IRS tax codes are littered with tax traps that retired and older Americans must deal with. Capital gains taxes, Social Security taxes, estate taxes, investment maturity taxes, and luxury taxes all bite into the average retiree's money. Saving money all the years that you have worked should not make you a target of even more taxes. Would our founding fathers have approved of taxation of those who are no longer employed? Isn't it unfair to expect people to keep paying fees to Uncle Sam for the money that will lead them into their elderly years?

Recently there has been some great huffing and puffing around Capitol Hill concerning senior citizen entitlement programs. No one wants to pay for them, no one wants to be left out of his or her fair share, and no one wants to be the one to tick off current seniors, who are a powerful voting bloc. Yet no one wants to talk about the financial problems facing senior entitlements, for fear of ridicule from seniors and their advocates. It is common knowledge in Congress that Social Security and Medicare are two of the great untouchable subjects when looking for constituent brownie points.

Unfortunately, it is an undeniable fact that when the Baby Boom generation eases into retirement, financial resources for senior entitlements will be strained beyond capacity. Although some Congressmen, such as Mark Neumann of Wisconsin and Gerald Solomon of Washington, are attempting to chip away at the intense shroud surrounding Social Security, nothing has happened yet to save the troubled program. Even though there are varying estimates on the impending bankruptcy of Social Security, the bottom line is that you can't really predict the future of the program.

When the Baby Boom generation retires, the ratio of taxpayers supporting Baby Boomers' Social Security needs will dwindle to three taxpayers to one beneficiary. The average Social Security check will be more than $1,000 a month. How will one taxpayer be able to part with over three hundred dollars every month? Your current Social Security payments are being used to finance government projects completely unrelated to Social Security, most especially to help deflate the deficit.

The government knows it is spending your retirement money, but it is legal. Some seniors' groups, such as the Seniors Coalition and the United Seniors Association, are attempting to bring to light the problem of these trust fund "raids." Although Congress says it is merely borrowing the money, and will return it when seniors need it, no one knows how it will come up with the money.

It is safe to say, then, that you are really on your own when it comes to planning for your retirement. With some savvy financial planning, a little flexibility, and some creativity, you can make the most of your retirement dollars. Read these strategies so that you avoid spending unnecessary money and take all the tax deductions you're entitled to.

Sell Your Home Tax-Free

The best way to sell your home is to sell it tax-free. A one-time IRS deduction is available for couples, of which one partner must be age 55 or more, to claim a $500,000 tax deduction from the sale of their home. You may claim $250,000 from the sale of your home if you are single. This is a deduction that can only occur every two years or more, and a sale that's a penny more than $250,000 or $500,000 is slapped with capital gains taxes.

Rent From Your Children Or Grandchildren

Your children can make tax deductions if they purchase a property for you and allow you to rent from them. They will receive deductions for property taxes and interest on the mortgage, and if they charge you "fair-market" rent; that is, rent that is appropriate for the neighborhood, amenities of the property, etc., then they can make depreciation deductions for the property as well.

Save Those Doctor's Notes!

Any medical expense of more than 7.5 percent of your adjusted gross income is tax deductible. While you might only qualify surgery or doctor's visits as income, the IRS validates doctors' notes for prescription or nonprescription medications as deductible medical expenses. For example, if your doctor has recommended that you take expensive nutritional supplements, herbal remedies or vitamins for your health, ask him to write that the expense is medically necessary and deduct the cost! This advice can apply to other medically necessary procedures as well, such as physical therapy, massages, or substance abuse programs. Other tax deductible procedures include couple's counseling, dentures, or health-related weight control programs. Even if you use aspirin, ask your doctor to write a note for you, because the costs do add up!

TAX SAVINGS FOR A SURVIVING SPOUSE

The law allows a surviving widow or widower to file lower joint-return tax rates for two years following the death of the spouse. You must have dependent children at home to qualify for this tax deduction, and file Form 1040.

HIGHER INCOME SOCIAL SECURITY BENEFIT TRAP

If you are in a higher income bracket, your Social Security benefits are taxed when you receive them. For a single recipient, incomes of $25,000 or more are taxed, and the amount for a couple is $50,000 or more (as of press time).

When you are in the work force and earning paychecks, your federal and state income taxes and your Social Security payments are taken from the gross amount. Then, when your Social Security check comes in the mail, you may be taxed again, depending on your income bracket. Thus, some people are taxed twice on their Social Security benefits.

There is no way to avoid this tax trap without some crafty investment or personal strategies. The total income that the government uses to tax your income is based not only on earned income but also on tax-free interest. One way to lower your paper income is to invest in assets that do not earn you immediate interest income. Or you can plan your investment earnings around times that you will have big deductions.

Another financially wise thing to do is check your Social Security earnings. It certainly does no harm to ask the Social Security Administration to check your earnings to make sure no mistakes have been made. Make sure that you keep your W-2s from work and check them against your statement. Unfortunately, you can only correct mistakes for about three years after they were made. A good habit to get into is to pick up form SSA 7004 from the Social Security Administration and send it in about every three years.

If you owe money to the IRS, your Social Security benefits will be levied. This will affect up to fifteen percent of your total benefit check. A word to the wise: pay your taxes!

IRA PLANNING

The Individual Retirement Account is a good retirement investment choice for some, but not for everyone. Consider that you can open a regular interest-bearing savings account for $1,000 and earn about $6,000 in interest over a ten-year period, assuming a five percent interest rate. You are paying taxes on the interest but you can withdraw money any time you need to. On the other hand, you can also start an IRA and put your money into the account tax-free., Depending on your income bracket, however, you will have to pay eight percent of your accumulated total in taxes when you withdraw the money. You might be better off just using your savings account to save money. Or, if your income bracket will be low when you collect your IRA earnings, you should consider utilizing the IRA since you will pay fewer tax dollars.

You can borrow money from your IRA indirectly. Within a sixty-day period, you can take money from one IRA, use it for your needs, then return the money to a different IRA without facing a penalty. This transfer is perfectly legal, but only one such transaction is allowed every twelve months.

ESTATE PLANNING

Citizens For A Sound Economy, a think-tank group based in Washington DC, recently published a policy newsletter entitled, "Even in Death the Tax Man Cometh." Truer words were never spoken. Even after the death of a loved one, Uncle Sam pays his respects by reaching into the pockets of the deceased one last time.

While estate planning can be a frustrating and arduous ordeal, you need to properly plan for your estate in order to pay the least amount of taxes, while benefiting from the maximum income potential. Unfortunately, not planning for tax payments means that the government will decide who pays the taxes from your pool of beneficiaries. Someone may have to pay dearly for merely being a beneficiary on your will. It is in your best interest to plan your estate taxes yourself.

Many states require beneficiaries to pay some estate taxes on their inheritance unless you stipulate otherwise in your will. Therefore, you should add to your will a clause ordering the payment of taxes from your residuary estate without apportionment. However, make sure that money donated to your spouse or to a charity, which will be tax-free, is not included in this statement. This way you will avoid taxes on would otherwise be a tax-free contribution. Carefully plan how your residuary estate money will be doled out to your beneficiaries. Make sure there is enough money to pay taxes after they receive their inheritance.

If you want to leave your children your home, but you still want to live in it, be prepared for a tax nightmare from the IRS. You would potentially owe a gift tax for bequeathing the home to your children and an estate tax because you maintained the home as a primary residence before your death. In order to avoid this, after you give your children your home, utilize the "Rent From Your Children" strategy described earlier in this chapter to save yourself exorbitant estate taxes. You then will only be taxed for the room you rented from your children.

Another potential problem to avoid is living or holding assets in more than one state. Although your accountant may tell you that all of your assets are in one state, check for yourself. A straggling tie to your old state can be a loss of money and a claim by your old state for a portion of estate taxes.

Also, make sure that you give someone you trust all of your tax return information. This person needs to know what deductions you took and why, have your documentation to prove it, and be able to defend you if the IRS audits you. It is a sad but true fact that the IRS has been known to seek out the tax returns of deceased individuals to see if they are owed any money. Those who cannot defend themselves are thus rendered helpless against IRS attack unless they have someone who can fight for them.

As a final note, remember that you can never plan too early for your estate. The National Audit Defense Network can look over your beneficiary lists, gifts, and assets and recommend to you the best approach to saving yourself tax dollars.

CHAPTER FOURTEEN

TAX STRATEGIES FOR THE FAMILY

It used to be that married couples enjoyed immense tax benefits. Those days are nearly gone, with recent tax code changes that all but eliminate the benefits of a dual-earning household. However, there are still a myriad of opportunities for tax savvy families just waiting to be tapped.

The economy of the 1990s has baffled financial planners, but certainly has been a boon to Mr. and Mrs. John Q. Taxpayer. Low inflation and brisk spending have been exhilarating for Americans of all income brackets, and our purchases and investments are at an all time high. No one can accurately predict when the honeymoon will be over, though, and with this in mind it is in the best interest of most Americans to save money for the future.

The following tax tips will help you plan your tax returns more wisely, and save money for those family vacations and college tuitions.

JOINT V. INDIVIDUAL TAX RETURNS

The gap between a husband's and a wife's earnings has diminished considerably in the past two decades. Today in many ways it is more cost-effective to stay single. Almost everyone has heard of the marriage tax penalty, which means that married couples pay more tax than non-married couples who earn approximately the same amount of money. Once upon a time there was a deduction available for dual-earner couples, but those days are gone, effective two years ago. However, if one spouse earns decidedly more than the other, the income difference will help in situations such as casualty loss, where the higher income helps raise the value of the loss, since you are allowed ten percent of your Adjusted Gross Income as a deduction.

The best way to know if you will owe more taxes filing jointly or separately is merely to figure it out both ways, with a pencil and paper, and then file whichever way is less costly for you. You can change your return up to three years after you've filed if you decide to file the other way after all, but if you figure everything out both ways ahead of time, you will probably not have to utilize this option.

The IRS currently only allows couples married under law to file joint returns. Gay or live-in couples may not file joint returns. Perhaps this will change in the next few years, but for now the IRS honors joint returns only from "traditional" couples.

Keep in mind that you are in part responsible for the actions of your spouse when he or she files a joint return for both of you. Since both partners sign the 1040, and you are bound by "joint and several liability," it is hard for an IRS agent to rightfully justify your excuse that your spouse filled out the return and you had no knowledge of his or her improper actions.

There have been countless cases of ex-husbands or wives who had no idea that their partner filed returns with improper deductions or flubbed-up math, and the IRS will look for ways to blame you for your spouse's mistake. There is a provision in the IRS tax code called the "innocent spouse" clause, and it does give you some protection against your spouse's false financial information, but it is limited in the protection it gives you. The IRS, without telling you about this provision, can ask you certain questions about your tax return, and if you answer a certain way, the agent may tell you that you cannot hide behind the innocent spouse provision.

Judith, a business executive with three children, is now on a payment plan with the IRS to pay taxes that her ex-husband never filed. Although Judith always reported her income properly on their joint tax returns, her husband misreported his income, and the IRS came after *her* to pay his taxes after their divorce. Judith is now more than $60,000 in debt to the IRS for deception that she had no knowledge of, and her ex-husband is now unemployed and "invisible" to the IRS. "It would do me absolutely no good to tell the IRS where he is, because he has no money anyway," Judith says. "The frustrating aspect of all of this is that I did nothing wrong. I was punished for my ex-husband's mistakes."

ADOPTED CHILD CREDIT

Couples who adopt a child are entitled to a $5,000 tax credit, provided their combined income is less than $75,000. Couples earning more than $75,000 will earn reduced credits, and those couples earning more than $115,000 per year receive no credit.

Expenses that qualify as a tax credit include almost every aspect of adoption, from court costs to legal fees to expenses associated with the adoption agency. If you adopt a disabled or mentally retarded child, your deduction increases by $1,000.

CLAIMING DEPENDENTS

When you claim a dependent on your 1040, you are receiving $2,500 credit on your taxes. The IRS will not give this amount away easily, and they may question your claim, so it is important to know who you can claim and why.

With extended families and stepfamilies on the rise, and with grandparents and elderly relatives living longer, the definition of a dependent has broadened for many taxpayers. So who qualifies as a dependent? Obviously, the immediate children of a taxpayer qualify as dependents, but many people do not know that other people whom you may support will qualify you for the deduction. A dependent is defined as someone who receives more than *half* of his or her financial support from the taxpayer. This person, if married, must not file a joint return and also must be your custodial dependent if you are divorced. Some court cases stipulate that the noncustodial parent has the right to claim the dependent, but this is not the norm and, in any event, it must be explicitly stated in whatever legal settlement you reach. If you want to switch the dependent claim to someone else, you must document this in writing every year in which you decide to do this.

A dependent can be a grandchild, stepchild, stepparent, parent, grandparent, sibling, in-law, niece or nephew, or any person living in your home for the entire year in a situation allowed by law (no harboring runaways or fugitives). You can also split responsibility for a dependent with others if you share financial responsibility for this person. For example, if you and your two sisters share financial responsibilities for your elderly father, you may fill out Form 2120 and receive the dependent deduction for your father's expenses. The only catch is that only one person may claim this deduction each year. The IRS does not mind if you claim the deduction one year and one of your sisters claims the deduction next year.

EDUCATIONAL TAX SAVINGS

Recently, thanks to the attention paid by Capitol Hill to the rising cost of education, you can declare some deductions for education. You are now allowed $1,000 credit for each child in higher education for the first year they are enrolled. The amount drops to $500 for the second year. You may claim the credit for not only a four-year university, but also for a two-year community college, or a vocational or trade school. The student must be enrolled throughout both semesters and be a legal dependent of the taxpayer who is claiming the deduction.

If you or your child receive scholarships or grants, the amount of the grant is completely tax-free, provided the money is spent on necessary educational supplies, such as books, tuition, fees, writing materials—even a computer for your child's homework and term papers! If you must perform a service at the institution for your scholarship, such as teach a class or do some administrative work, then the aid becomes completely taxable, regardless of how you spend it.

DIVORCE CAN BE COSTLY

The IRS will not shed a tear for you when they discover that your blissful wedded days are over. Rather, they will have their hand out just like your ex when it comes time to divvy up the goods. However, the IRS can be lenient when it comes to some payments; it's important to know where you stand on the tax line with various financial payments.

During this time it is difficult to think about what will happen when it's time to file next year's 1040, but at the time of the separation and divorce more than any other time you must keep detailed and accurate records of every transaction that takes place, and discuss with your accountant or attorney the financial preparations you will need to make above and beyond your usual plan of action.

Alimony payments are completely tax deductible for the payer but are income for the payee. You must ensure that your payments actually look like alimony. Your payments must be in equal installments and over an evenly distributed amount of time. When you receive alimony, you must ensure that you report the amount as income and pay the appropriate taxes on it.

Property that was part of your divorce settlement is tax deductible. If you make mortgage payments or maintenance costs as part of your divorce settlement, however, you may deduct these costs as part of alimony. Child support is not tax deductible, either. Child support does not count as income for the recipient, but the payer cannot deduct the amount from his or her taxes.

Overall, the benefits for the average middle-class family are dwindling. However, with the right informational tools, you can save considerable tax dollars.

CHAPTER FIFTEEN

THE PROSPECTS FOR TAX REFORM

WHY THE CURRENT SYSTEM HAS TO GO

Every taxpaying American, and that includes those of us as young as one-year-old, has personal experiences with the Internal Revenue Service and the intricacies and complexity of its tax code. We all instinctively know that there has to be a better way. But for those who require more than a gut feeling, political scientist James L. Payne has done the most comprehensive—and irrefutable—job of delineating the burdens and distortions of the current tax system (*Costly Returns*, Institute for Contemporary Studies, 1993).

In a nutshell, his findings, for the year 1985, are as follows:

Compliance costs

	Billion
Businesses	$102.3
Individuals	57.1

Enforcement costs

	Billion
Initial contacts	5.5
Tax litigation	3.4
Forced collections	4.0
Disincentives to production	155.3
Disincentive cost of tax uncertainty	12.0
Evasion and avoidance cost	19.3
Governmental costs	4.0
Total	$362.9

Even more startling than the gross figure revealed by this table is the fact that it totals 65 percent of the available revenue collected. In other words, it costs 65 cents to collect one dollar of revenue!

The economic and personal reality of this gross waste and abusive power lies at the heart of the current tax revolt and the push for simplification. This chapter examines the major alternatives to the current system, and the prospects for reform in the immediate future.

In theory, there is a broad agreement on the characteristics of a good system of taxation. The National Commission on Economic Growth and Taxation, which finished its work only this year, established twelve criteria for an ideal tax system.

A. SIX PRINCIPLES

1. An ideal system must provide incentives to work, save and invest, in order to promote economic growth.

2. An ideal system must be fair to all taxpayers.

3. An ideal system will be simple, so that any taxpayer can figure out his own taxes.

4. An ideal system will be neutral. It will not bias the choices individuals make about their income-producing activities, or about their expenditures. In other words, the individual will make choices, not the government.

5. An ideal tax will be visible, so that people will know the true cost of government.

6. An ideal system will be stable, so that people can plan for the future.

B. SIX POINTS OF POLICY

1. There will be a single tax rate. It is well-recognized that one of the worst evils of our present system is that it taxes income more than once, leading to inequities, confusions, economic, distortion, and cheating.

2. There will be a generous personal exemption, removing the burden on those least able to pay. Of course this policy position conflicts with point two above.

3. Tax rates will be lower for all American families.

4. The new tax system will include the deductibility of payroll taxes such as Social Security and Medicare.

5. The bias against work, savings, and investment will be ended.

6. The new, ideal system will be hard to change, probably by requiring a super majority in Congress for any changes.

While there are still adamant egalitarians among us who want to use the tax code to redistribute wealth and income and, while there are social engineers who want to use the mechanisms of the tax code to bring about specific societal outcomes, these forces are in retreat. It appears that the question, at long last, is not will we reform the tax code from top to bottom, but when, and which among a number of attractive alternatives will we choose.

ALTERNATIVES TO THE PRESENT SYSTEM OF TAXATION

1. A FLAT TAX

Popularized by presidential candidate Steve Forbes in the 1996 campaign, the most influential version of the flat tax was devised by Hoover Institution economists Alvin Rabushka and Robert Hall, and introduced in legislative form by Rep. Dick Armey of Texas and Sen. Richard Shelby of Alabama. Essentially, the Hall-Rabushka flat tax replaces the present tax code with a single tax rate of seventeen percent. The proposal includes a generous family allowance of $33,300 for a family of four, effectively removing all lower-income families from the tax roles, and preserving a slight-progressivity in the tax code.

The tax is collected in two ways: wages, salaries, and other earnings are reported by individuals on a tax return essentially the size of a postcard. Earnings on interest and investment income are calculated and paid by the business entity, and the return on investment to the individual is reduced by that amount.

It should be obvious that so-called "unearned income"—income earned by the investment of capital—is indeed taxed, but apparently the point is not obvious. One can excuse presidential candidate Robert Dole (with difficulty) for making this mistake, because although he has years of experience on the Senate tax-writing committee, he is not a trained economist. It is much harder to justify presidential candidate Phil Gramm's attack on the Hall-Rabushka plan. In any event, let me repeat: investment income is taxed to the individual, but the tax is calculated, withheld, and paid by the company or investment entity producing the income. In this way, all income, whether "earned" or "unearned" is taxed at the same rate and taxed only once.

Exempt from taxation would be all savings, including money invested either in securities or in a business. In that way, the Hall-Rabushka flat tax is a tax only on consumed income, although it is rarely described in that way.

While probably the simplest of all the alternatives to the current system, there are some political liabilities to a flat tax. One is that it is vulnerable to the (untrue) charge that while wage income is taxed, investment income is not.

A second political disadvantage is that the pure flat tax, as envisioned by Hall and Rabushka, would eliminate all current deductions from taxable income, including the politically popular home mortgage deduction and charitable contributions. Proponents of Hall-Rabushka do not accept these criticisms. They argue that the decline in mortgage rates that would accompany the flattening of rates would more than compensate for the value of the deduction, which is generally of more benefit to the rich anyway. As for the charitable contribution deduction, they point out that charitable contributions are rarely made in order to escape taxation, and that leaving more disposable income with taxpayers is the best way to encourage charitable contributions. Nonetheless, the recognition of the political potency of these deductions has led to the introduction of modified flat tax bills, such as that of Sen. Arlen Specter of Pennsylvania, which would retain those two deductions, in exchange for slightly higher tax rates.

In any event, elimination of the mortgage deduction especially could not be done in a single stroke. There would have to be transition rules of some kind. That is also true of the major competitors of the flat tax, such as the national sales tax. Additionally, since there would have to be some judgments made as to the distinctions between consumption and investment, the flat tax cannot offer the promise of the total elimination of the IRS. On the other hand, it is my opinion that the other alternatives can make no such claim either, as we will see.

2. A NATIONAL SALES TAX

The elimination of the Internal Revenue Service is one of the most potent political issues in America today. As the recent hearings before the Senate Finance Committee conclusively demonstrated, the IRS is indeed a rogue agency, and if every taxpaying American has not felt its wrath, irrationality and arbitrariness, they have close friends or relatives who have. Our opinion is that it is this hatred of the IRS that drives the case for a national sales tax.

The leading exponent of the national sales tax is Rep. Billy Tauzin of Alabama in the House, aided and abetted by the Chairman of the House Ways and Means Committee, Bill Archer of Texas. As introduced in the House, the national sales tax bill would completely eliminate all taxes on income, and replace them with a retail sales tax, levied on the end-use purchaser. The libertarian-oriented Cato Institute in Washington favors a national sales tax, and has an organized campaign to promote it nationwide.

The details of the operation of any national sales tax remain somewhat murky, as a number of questions have not been answered. For example, a national sales tax is regressive, in that the purchase of basic necessities such as food, clothing, and shelter, consume a much higher percentage of the disposable income of poor people than they do for those who are better off. Accordingly, most sales tax proposals exempt from the tax basic commodities such as food and drugs. Others rebate to lower-income workers an amount designed to protect them from the worst effects of this progressivity.

Immediately, one begins to see the IRS arising from the ashes, phoenix-like. Someone must make a determination of what goods and services are basic, and so exempt from tax. There would also be a temptation to use any such tax exemptions to further social policy. Under current political conditions, cigarettes would certainly be taxed, but what about potato chips and Twinkies? Are they vital food stuffs or unnecessary fluff? And how about greasy and unhealthful hamburgers? Political battles lie in wait.

Alternatively, if the decision is made to rebate to the poor, someone must determine who is poor and so qualifies for the rebate. The federal government provides many services to the poor, on a means-tested basis. We may not like these programs, but they are there, and no proposed sales tax bill proposes to repeal them. Someone has to determine who is eligible for means-tested assistance, and that requires record-keeping, investigations, and enforcement. Again, the IRS is back on the job, whatever it might be called.

Other problems exist with a national sales tax. For example, proponents often claim that it would be easy to administer, because it would simply be added to the sales tax already in effect in the states. But there is no sales tax in five states. Would they be required to enact one? It is curious to see libertarians who favor a sales tax so quick to require the imposition of a tax on citizens of a state who do not have one.

And what about revenue effects? We are not enamored of the "revenue neutral" requirement so dear to the hearts of big-government liberals, but let us assume that government expenditures will continue at roughly the same level of GDP as today. In that case, the sales tax rate would have to exceed twenty percent and, at that level, smuggling, the cash economy, and other forms of tax evasion become attractive. In order to avoid them, the sales tax is pushed down the production chain, becoming a Value Added Tax (see next section).

It is often argued that a sales tax would capture revenue now being lost in the "underground economy," as drug lords and crime figures would have to pay taxes on the things they buy. However, the primary attraction of the underground economy is its invisibility from law enforcement for illicit activity. A prostitute is not going to charge sales tax on her services, and plumbers and others who want to operate in an untaxed cash economy would continue to have an incentive to do so. In fact, if the sales tax rate were higher than twenty percent, the underground economy might well grow.

Two other quick points. The sales tax offers one of the bleakest prospects the tax reformer can imagine: a tax system with both a sales tax and an income tax. In fact, there is no known example of a government simply replacing an income tax with a sales tax. Unless the enactment of a sales tax is accompanied by constitutional safeguards against a

concommitant income tax, it will suffer insurmount-
able political opposition.

Only slightly less dire is the prospect of a hidden
tax, one whose rates can easily be jacked up an
eighth of a percentage point every time a
big-spending politician dreams up a new federal
spending program.

3. A VALUE ADDED TAX

The VAT is really nothing more than a sales tax,
but one that is imposed at each stage of production,
and paid on the value added to the goods at each
stage. For example, a lumberjack pays a tree farmer
$100 for the right to cut down a tree. The tree farmer
pays a twenty percent tax on the $100. The
lumberjack sells the tree to a mill for $150, paying a
twenty percent tax on the $50 in value he added to
it. The mill cuts the tree into rough lumber and sells
it to a furniture manufacturer for $500, paying
twenty percent on the $400 in value added. The
furniture manufacturer converts the wood into fine
furniture and sells it to a retail outlet for $1,000,
paying twenty percent on the $500 in value added.
Finally, the retailer sells the furniture to a customer
for $2,000, paying twenty percent on the $1,000 in
value added. Without the tax, the final price of the
furniture in this example would have been $1,595,
so it is obvious that it is the final consumer paying
the tax, but the tax was levied and collected and
paid over the course of the manufacturing cycle.

The amount of record-keeping leaps immediately to view in this example, as does the fact that

the true cost of taxation is well-hidden from the consumer.

Additional problems arise because the VAT is really only a sales tax, and so suffers the same disadvantages of regressivity and evasion that characterize that proposal. Also, in the history of the world, no VAT has ever been kept low; and virtually every country that has a VAT also has an income tax.

4. REVENUE TARIFFS

There is a small movement afoot to eliminate all income and sales taxes, and fund the government entirely out of tariffs levied on imported goods. A small number of economists endorse this approach, which is fueled mostly by a literal reading of the Constitution.

Because these tariffs would be imposed only for purposes of raising revenue, they would not vary from product to product, as tariffs often do today, and they would not be levied for the purposes of protecting infant industries or retaliating against restrictive trade partners. Thus, they would be relatively neutral in an economic sense, raising prices to all consumers by some percentage, just as all taxes do. They would discriminate against imports, of course, and thus invite retaliation, but they would not, as is often claimed, force foreigners to fund our government. Tariffs are paid by consumers in the form of higher prices, and thus Americans would bear the brunt of this taxation.

Advocates of revenue tariffs are usually strict constitutionalists who see very few functions of government as legitimate, so the prospect of minimal returns from such tariffs does not usually trouble them. Practical politicians, who want to know how to collect enough money to keep government at something near its present size, see different problems. Although little actual calculating has been done, in order to produce something like the current level of $1.5 trillion in revenue annually, the revenue tariff rate would have to be in excess of 100 percent, more than doubling prices of goods imported and exported. Of course, at that level, imports would fall, leading to lower revenues, higher rates, lower imports, and so on in a death spiral. The reaction of our trading partners can only be imagined, but it would undoubtedly end export prospects.

PROSPECTS

The debate over the nature of taxation is, in our opinion, now well underway. The 1996 presidential campaign got the ball rolling, and the IRS oversight hearings of September 1997 helped a lot. Specific legislation has been introduced, and Representatives Dick Armey (for the flat tax) and Billy Tauzin (for the NST) have begun a road show that promises to further educate the public. Steve Forbes, the leading advocate of a flat tax at the presidential level promises to be a factor in the year 2000, but even before that there are likely to be debates and perhaps test votes in Congress leading up to the congressional elections of 1998.

One test may come on legislation similar to that recently introduced by Rep. Steve Largent of Oklahoma, whose bill would sunset the entire tax code on 31 December 2001, essentially giving Congress until then to come up with something better. Rep. Bill Paxon of New York has initiated a similar bill that would sunset everything but Social Security and Medicare, a year earlier. The Republican House leadership has shown some interest in these proposals, and in the interest of furthering the tax debate, may bring one or more of them to a vote in the second session of the 105th Congress. With Bill Clinton in the White House, no such proposal could pass, but that fact might even make a vote less risky and thus a positive vote more likely.

Our guess is that the tax code will be a major—perhaps even the defining issue in the presidential campaign of 2000, and that shortly after the election, we will see the enactment of a tax which is flatter, fairer, and simpler. In short, we are now debating how to tax consumption rather than income, and what the collection mechanism will be. The debate over whether or not we will eliminate the current income tax system is over.

CHAPTER SIXTEEN

WHAT IS THE NATIONAL AUDIT DEFENSE NETWORK?

A continuing problem for the IRS is how to determine whether people in tip-based careers, such as bartenders, casino game dealers and waiters, tell the truth on their tax returns. Not only does the cash aspect of the business make tracing earnings extremely difficult, but the actual customer flow and tips generated fluctuate wildly from day to day for many employees. Variations in tip earnings on any particular day include not only the customer count but also the personality of the employee, the personality of the customer, the socioeconomic status of the customer, the time of day, the amount of the bill to tip on, and plain old luck.

If a blackjack dealer just happens to win for the casino most of his shift, he will probably not generate many tips. Also, almost every type of cash-based career has several tiers of prestige; a waiter at a pancake house will not make the same amount of money that a waiter at a popular bar and grill will make, who will not make what a waiter at a four-star French restaurant will make. There are geographical considerations as well and, of course, there are circumstances beyond the control of the tip earner that may affect their earnings anyway: a bad cook, a crying baby in the restaurant, a poor hand in poker. In spite of the unstable nature of a career with tips for the majority of an employee's earnings, the IRS nonetheless attempted to quantify what earnings might be for such groups.

In the late 1970s, the IRS began a campaign to target casino dealers. They arrived in Reno, Nevada, a hotbed of dealers, and infiltrated the casino world. Revenue agents set up camp in a major casino in order to get an idea of how much money an average person in such a field would earn in tips on a particular night. The agents came up with an equation that would determine the typical amount a dealer should write on his or her 1040. Any person not in the income bracket they had determined would be the potential target of an audit.

Casino employees who got wind of this plan began to panic. How exactly can you prove cash earnings? And if they were well above or below the IRS equation, who would believe that they had a slow or busy month? The dealers were justifiably terrified, and so they contacted Mr. Pat Cavanaugh.

THE LEGACY OF PAT CAVANAUGH'S PREPAID AUDIT DEFENSE

Pat Cavanaugh is a former IRS agent from Lake Tahoe, Nevada who decided to specialize in audit defense for taxpayers. As a former agent, he knew the tactics and the ins and outs of IRS audits, and his business had a ninety-five percent success rate. His accounting practice was gaining renown as *the* place to go to get honest, hard-fought victories against the IRS. Pat's philosophy was to, "pull the tight rope of IRS deductions so tight it's taut, and then you can walk across it with courage; but don't let it break, or you'll fall every time."

Reno casino employees called Cavanaugh in 1979 and told him of their dilemma. Any of them could be a target of IRS attack. What should they do? They wanted to benefit from his audit defense business but could not afford the expensive rates he normally charged. Cavanaugh decided that the best way to handle the situation was to pool together funds and call it the "Audit Defense Fund." Then, if one of the casino employees was audited, he could use the common fund to defend his audit. Much like auto or home insurance, they purchased audit insurance. Someone who was audited got several hundred or thousands of dollars worth of audit defense for only their membership fee.

It didn't take long before Cavanaugh's prepaid audit defense network expanded beyond the casino world. Soon the network included small business owners, entertainers, doctors, marketers and other business people throughout the West. Cavanaugh was gaining increasing clout in financial circles as the force to contend with when dealing with the IRS. His business continued to flourish, and he began to envision a national network of thousands of members who could force the IRS to treat taxpayers ethically. He named his company Advanced Tax Representation, Inc. and set up a Board of Advisers and a headquarters staff.

Cavanaugh succeeded tremendously in his goal. He has countless stories of taxpayers in trouble who were being harassed by IRS agents. As soon as he stepped in to take care of the situation, the agents, recognizing him as a former agent and knowledgeable tax strategist, often resolved problems immediately. Cavanaugh has reintroduced people into the tax system after they had been invisible for years, has negotiated deals with agents, and has closed cases in favor of his clients when it seemed certain that the IRS would win. Cavanaugh's crusade to save the American taxpayer continued to flourish, until a troubling event occurred in the mid 1980s.

Cavanaugh decided to produce an infomercial that showed people how IRS revenue agents can go overboard when trying to collect taxes. His intention was not only to solicit business but also to generate a public outcry regarding the abuses of the IRS. He recalled the story of a quadriplegic who owed the IRS several thousand dollars. In this actual case, the man had no other assets left to be taken by revenue agents, so they took his wheelchair. He filmed the scene, and not long after the infomercial aired, the IRS was inundated with angry calls. Panicking, the IRS met with Cavanaugh, and after several heated meetings, Cavanaugh and the IRS agreed to terms of dealing with each other that are still in effect today. Cavanaugh would pull the infomercial in return for the ability to continue his Audit Defense Network. He would also be allowed to say anything he wanted about the IRS as a former agent and audit defender, but would not be allowed to publicly slander the agency or disclose certain taxpayer information, even if the taxpayer approved the use of it.

Cavanaugh continued his audit defense practice until he was diagnosed with diabetes in the early 1990s. His condition worsened to the point that it became difficult for him to continue the grueling schedule that heading a pre-paid audit company required. In 1994 he sold his business to associates who unfortunately unraveled much of Cavanaugh's hard work. They did not continue to cultivate membership or aggressively defend audits, and by late 1995 the organization was in trouble.

Then, in January 1996, two men, Robert Bennington and Cort Christie, the authors of this book, acted on their desire to carry on Cavanaugh's legacy by buying the company and renaming it the National Audit Defense Network. Bennington and Christie brought together two sides of the business world: Bennington as an experienced salesperson who would help solicit and maintain membership, and Christie as a small business owner adept in tax strategies. The National Audit Defense Network was thus re-formed to continue Cavanaugh's legacy of inexpensive, high quality audit defense while adding membership benefits to make the network a financial asset to Americans while generating growth and visibility in the community once again.

Response to the National Audit Defense Network in the past twenty-four months has been overwhelming. Membership has grown almost 1,000 percent as of September 1997 and is expected to hit almost 2,000 percent growth by tax season 1998. Executive offices in Las Vegas have grown from six employees to twenty-four and with a network of more than 1,000 former IRS agents, CPAs and accountants, the organization has flourished again.

1997 also was a stellar year for NADN as the company continued to build influence and visibility throughout the country. NADN representatives were granted Power of Attorney by Ms. Paula Jones and her husband for their audit, an audit which has been extremely controversial, since the audit notice arrived only days after Ms. Jones rejected President Clinton's sexual harrassment settlement.

NADN president Robert Bennington has introduced the organization to the media; during the last week of September alone his expertise on the IRS and taxation led to appearances on CNN, the *Jim Lehrer News Hour*, the *G. Gordon Liddy Show*, the *Mary Matalin Show*, the *Oliver North Show*, the *Chuck Harter Show*, NET Television, and CNBC. Mary Matalin declared on her show that she was immediately joining NADN, and that the company "renewed her faith" in the tax system.

Dr. Arthur Green, a dentist and NADN member in suburban Maryland who was himself an IRS abuse victim, became a vital NADN and IRS reform spokesperson during the week of the Senate Finance Committee hearings in Congress. He appeared on CNN and on the *Oliver North Show* to discuss his case and show how the average person can become an IRS statistic.

Currently, membership in the National Audit Defense Network includes not only free representation for audits, but also a quarterly newsletter, a toll-free tax question hotline, updates on current and future changes in the tax code, and tips for filling out tax returns.

More than ever before, Cavanaugh's legacy now lives on.

It is unfortunate that there need to be watchdogs for the agency that collects our taxes. Groups on both sides of politics and even Congress itself have fortunately begun to look at the "IRS Mess," and propose solutions for our future. In September 1997 the Senate Finance Committee, chaired by Senator William Roth, conducted pivotal hearings on IRS abuses. IRS employees in disguise confirmed stories of intimidation, pressure, and outright lying to taxpayers to force them to pay extra taxes. Taxpayers themselves talked about losing everything they had, including their jobs, to pay the IRS on disputed and often false claims. Finally, IRS abuses are coming to light in the media and on Capitol Hill.

We hope that one day we can be proud of the Internal Revenue Service, rather than remain fearful of its unharnessed power to invade the lives and finances of taxpayers.

In an interview for this book, Cavanaugh told us that to this day, he firmly believes in the goals and vision of the National Audit Defense Network and what it can do for American taxpayers. "I have always felt that pre-paid audit defense is the most innovative idea for the average American. I never tire of helping people; the most gratifying reason to be a part of pre-paid audit defense is to hear the success stories. I will never get bored hearing about people who have put their feet back on the ground, and stood up to the IRS, with our help."

CHAPTER SEVENTEEN

TAX REFORM RESOURCE GUIDE

All of the organizations listed below can provide information about taxation, and about tax reform efforts, but their orientations may vary widely. Some of them can provide information only; others are lobbying organizations actively working to reform the tax code. Most of them are national organizations, wherever they may be located, but we have tried to include at least one organization for each of the fifty states (we have not quite succeeded), so that a taxpayer need not feel alone wherever located. Because in small organizations officers change often, and in large organizations there may be more than one expert available, we have not included specific names as contact points

As always, every effort has been made to make this information accurate, and we apologize in advance for any errors.

Alabama Family Alliance
402 Office Park Dr., Suite 300
Birmingham AL 35223
(205) 870-9900
FAX (205) 8704407
alfamillia@aol.com

Alabama Taxpayers Association
3472 Bankhead Ave.
Montgomery, AL 36111
(334) 409-3119

Alaskans for Tax Reform
2509 Eide St., Suite 4
Anchorage, AL 99503
(907) 258-8888

Alexis de Tocqueville Institute
1611 No. Kent St., Suite 901
Arlington, VA 22209
(703) 351-4969
(703) 351-0090 FAX

American Council for Capital Formation
1750 K St., N.W., Suite 400
Washington, DC 20006
(202) 293-5811
(202) 785-8165 FAX

American Enterprise Institute
1150 17th St., N.W.
Washington, DC 20036
(202) 862-5800
(202) 862-7178 FAX

American Institute for Economic Research
534 Cary Drive
Auburn, AL
(334) 887-5957
(334) 887-6461 FAX

American Legislative Exchange Council
910 17th St., N.W., 5th Floor
Washington, DC 20006
(202) 466-3800
(202) 466-3801 FAX

Americans for Tax Reform
1320 18th St., N.W., Suite 200
Washington, DC 20036
(202) 785-0266
(202) 785-0261 FAX

Arizona: *See* Lincoln Caucus

Arkansas: *See* Taxpayers Rights Committee

Arkansas Policy Foundation
8201 Cantrell Rd., Suite 325
Little Rock, AR 72227
(501) 227-4815
(501) 227-8970 FAX

aggiemw2@aol.com

Atlantic Institute for Market Studies
1326 Barrington St.
Halifax, Nova Scotia B3J 1Z1 CANADA
(902) 429-1143
(902) 423-1528 FAX
aims@fox.nstn.ca

Beacon Hill Institute
8 Ashburton Place
Boston, MA 02108
(617) 573-8750
(617) 720-4272 FAX

Californians for Tax Reform
250 First St., Suite 330
Claremont, CA 91711
(909) 621-6825

Cascade Policy Institute
16055-B, S.W. Boones Ferry Rd., Suite 380
Lake Oswego, OR 97035
(503) 598 4463
(503) 598-4414 info@cascadepolicy.com

Cato Institute
1000 Massachusetts Ave., N.W.
Washington, DC 20001
(202) 842-0200
(202) 842-3490 FAX

Center for the Study of Public Choice
MSN 1D3
George Mason University
Fairfax, VA 22030
(703) 993-2331
(703) 522-4952 FAX

Center for the Study of Market Processes
4084 University Dr., Suite 208
Fairfax, VA 22030
(703) 934-6970
(703) 934-1578 FAX
j.ellig@gmu.edu

Citizens Against Higher Taxes
P O Box 249
Annville, PA 17003
(717) 867-5491

Citizens for a Sound Economy
1250 H Street, N.W., Suite 700
Washington, DC 20005
(202) 783-3870
(202 783-4687 FAX

Citizens for Limited Taxation
1818 Tremont St., Rm. 608
Boston, MA 02108
(617) 248-0022

Claremont Institute
250 West First St., Suite 330
Claremont, CA 91711
(909) 621-6825
(909) 626-8724 FAX

Coalition of New York Taxpayers
31 Union Ave.
Center Moriches, NY 11934
(516) 878-3109

Coalition of Taxpayers (Hawaii)
Hawaii KAI Corporate
6600 Kalaninahole Hwy.
Honolulu, HI 96825
(808) 396-1724

Coalition of Taxpayers (Ohio)
3289 Rochford Ridge Dr.
Hilliard, OH 43221
(614) 777-4071

Coalition of Taxpayers (Virginia)
P O. Box 16436
Alexandria, VA 22302

Competitive Enterprise Institute
1001 Connecticut Ave., N.W. Suite 1250
Washington, DC 20036
(202) 331-1010
(202) 331-0640 FAX

Concerned Taxpayers (Mississippi)
P.O. Box 700
Magee, MS 39111
(601) 849-2210

Consumer Alert
1001 Connecticut Ave., N.W., Suite 1128
Washington, DC 20036
(202) 467-5809
(202) 467-5814 FAX
calert@his.com

Delaware: See Taxpayers Coalition

Empire Foundation for Policy Research
4 Chelsea Place
Clifton Park NY 12065
(518) 383-2877
(518) 383-2841 FAX

Employee Benefit Research Institute
2121 K Street, N.W., Suite 600
Washington, DC 20037
(202) 659-0670
(202) 775-6312 FAX

Empower America
1776 Eye St., N.W., Suite 800
Washington, DC 20006
(202) 452-8200
(202) 833-0388 FAX

Ethan Allen Institute
RR. 1, Box 43
Concord, VT 05824
(802) 695-1448
ethallen@plainfield.bypass.com

Evergreen Freedom Foundation
P.O. Box 552
Olympia, WA 98507
(360) 956-3482
(360) 352-1874 FAX

Family Research Council
801 G Street, N.W.
Washington, DC 20001
(202) 393-2100
(202) 393-2134 FAX

Fiscal Associates
1515 Jefferson Davis Hwy.
Arlington, VA 22202
(703) 413-4371
(703) 413-0280 garobbins@worldnet.att.net

Florida: See Tax Cap Committee

Florida Tax Watch
P.O. Box 10209
Tallahassee, FL 32302
(904) 222-5052
(904) 222-7476 FAX

Foundation for Economic Education
30 South Broadway
Irvington, NY 10533
(914) 591-7230
(914) 591-8910 FAX

Fraser Institute
626 Bute St., 2nd Floor
Vancouver, British Columbia
V6E 3M1 Canada
(604) 688-0221
(604) 688-8539 FAX

Georgia: See Taxpayers Network

Granite State Taxpayers
P O Box 10473
Bedford, NH 03110
(603) 472-3421

Hands Across New Jersey
612 Mountain Ave.
Bound Brook, NJ 08805
(908) 756-7094

Hawaii: See Coalition of Taxpayers

Heritage Foundation
214 Massachusetts Avenue, N.E.
Washington, DC 20002
(202) 546 4400
(202) 544-5421 FAX

Howard Jarvis Taxpayers Association
621 So. Westmoreland Ave., Suite 202
Los Angeles, CA 90005
(213) 384-9656
(213) 384-9870 FAX

Hudson Institute
1015 18th St., N.W., Suite 200
Washington, DC 20036
(202) 223-7770
(202) 223-8537 FAX
74170.3211@compuserve.com

Illinois: See Tax Accountability

Independent Institute
134 98th Ave.
Oakland, CA 94603
(510) 632-1366
(510) 568-6040 FAX
independent@dnai.com

Indiana Family Institute
70 East 91st St., Suite 210
Indianapolis, IN 46240
(317) 582-0300

Institute for Political Economy
505 So. Fairfax St.
Alexandria, VA 22314
(202) 686-6380
(202) 686-1726 FAX

Institute for Research of the Economics of Taxation
1300 19th St., N.W., Suite 240
Washington, DC 20036
(202) 463-1400
(202) 463-6199 FAX

International Tax and Investment Center
1250 H St., N.W., Suite 750
Washington, DC 20005
(202) 942-7651
(202) 942-7678 FAX

Iowans for Tax Relief
P.O. Box 747
Muscatine, IA 52761
(319) 264-8080
(319) 264-2413 FAX

John Locke Foundation
1304 Hillsborough St.
Raleigh, NC 27606
(919) 828-3876
(919) 821 -5117 FAX
locke@interpath.com

Kansas: See Taxpayer Network

Kentucky: See Taxpayers United

Lincoln Caucus
P.O. Box 9854
Phoenix, AZ 85056
(602) 248-0136

Louisianans for Tax Reform
227 Baxter Road
Ruston LA 71270
(318) 247-3744

Ludwig von Mises Institute
415 West Magnolia Ave., Suite 105
Auburn AL 36849
(334) 844-2500
(334) 844-2583 FAX

Mackinac Center for Public Policy
P.O. Box 568
Midland, Ml 48640
(517) 631-0900
(517) 631-0964
folsom@mackinac.org

Maine Tax Watch
P.O. Box 10
Garland, ME 04939
(207) 924-3835

Manhattan Institute for Policy Research
52 Vanderbilt Ave.
New York, NY 10017
(212) 599-7000
(212) 599 3494

Maryland Taxpayers Coalition
4321 Hartwick Road
College Park, MD 20740
(301) 699-9880

Massachusetts: See Citizens for Limited
Taxation

Michiganders for Tax Reform
1315 Westview #10
East Lansing, MI 48823
(517) 373-5228

Minnesota Family Council
2855 Anthony Lane So., Suite 150
Minneapolis, MN 55418
(612) 789-8811

Mississippi: See Concerned Taxpayers

Missourians for Tax Reform
1 Metropolitan Square, Suite 2600
St. Louis, MO 63102
(314) 621-5070

Momtanans for Tax Reform
4525 Highway 12
Helena, MT 59601
(406) 442-6682

National Center for Policy Analysis
12655 No. Central Expressway, Suite 720
Dallas, TX 75243
(972) 386-6272
(972) 386-0924
jgoodman@ncpa.public.policy.org

National Tax Limitation Committee
151 No. Sunrise Avenue, Suite 901
Roseville, CA 95611
(916) 786-9400
(916) 786-8163 FAX

National Taxpayers Union
108 North Alfred St.
Alexandria, VA 22314
(703) 683-5700
(703) 683-5722 FAX

Nevada Policy Research Institute
P.O. Box 20312
Reno, NV 89515
(702) 786-9600
(702) 786-9604 FAX
npri@policy.reno.nv.us

New Hampshire: See Granite State Taxpayers

New Jersey: See Hands Across New Jersey

New Mexico: See Tax Limitation

New York: See Coalition of New York Taxpayers

North Carolina: See Taxpayers United

North Dakota for Tax Reform
P. O. Box 1473
Bismarck, ND 58502
(701) 222-4860

NOVECON
1020 16th St., N.W., Suite 200
Washington, DC 20036
(202) 659-3200
(202) 659-3215 FAX
novmftco@aol.com

Ohio: See Coalition of Taxpayers

Ohio Roundtable
31005 Solon Road
Solon, OH 44139
(216) 349-3393
(216) 349-0154 FAX

Oklahoma for Tax Reform
P.O. Box 700255
Oklahoma City, OK 73107
(405) 947-2462

Oregon: See Taxpayers United

Pacific Research Institute
755 Sansome St., Suite 450
San Francisco, CA 94111
(415) 989-0833
(415) 989-2411 FAX

Pennsylvania. See Citizens Against Higher Taxes

Rhode Island Taxpayers
301 Friendship St.
Providence, RI 02903
(401) 351-0787

Rockford Institute
934 North Main St.
Rockford, IL 61103
(815) 964-5053
(815) 965-1826 FAX
rkfdinst@bossnt.com

Savers and Investors League
457 Inverary
Villanova, PA 19085
(610) 989 3970
(610) 98903972 FAX

Small Business Survival Committee
1320 18th St, N.W., Suite 200
Washington, DC 20036
(202) 785-0238
(202) 822-8118 FAX

South Carolina Policy Council
1419 Pendleton St.
Columbia, SC 29201
(803) 799-5022

Sutherland Institute
Independence Square
111 East 5600 South, Suite 208
Murray, UT 84107
(801) 281-2081
(801) 281-2414 FAX

Tax Accountability
59 E Van Buren St., Suite 2517
Chicago, IL 60605
(312) 427-5128

Tax Cap Committee
P.O. Box 193
New Smyrna Beach, FL 32170
(904) 423-4744

Tax Foundation
1250 H St., N.W., Suite 750
Washington, DC 20005
(202) 942-7681

Tax Limitation
1215 Los Arboles, N.W.
Albuquerque, NM 87107
(505) 828-4068

Taxpayer Network (Kansas)
P.O. Box 20050
Wichita, KS 67208
(316) 684 0082

Taxpayers Coalition (Delaware)
756 Auburn Mill Road
Hockessin, DE 19707
(302) 234-9815

Taxpayers Network (Georgia)
1234 Powers Ferry Road
Marietta, GA 30067
(404) 607-2254

Taxpayers Rights Committee
Central Mall Plaza, Suite 516
5111 Rogers Ave.
Fort Smith, AR 72903
(501) 452-3714

Taxpayers United (Kentucky)
2705 Utah Drive
Bowling Green, KY 42102
(502) 781-4909

Taxpayers United (North Carolina)
3901 Barren Drive, Suite 100
Raleigh, NC 27609
(919) 571-1441

Taxpayers United (Oregon)
8304 S.E. Stark
Portland, OR 97216
(503) 251-1635

Texas for Limited Taxation
P.O. 56767
Houston, TX 77256
(713) 684 6444

Thomas Jefferson Institute for Public Policy
8107 Long Shadows Drive
Fairfax Station, VA 22039
(703) 690-6333
(703) 690-5763 FAX

Utah: See Sutherland Foundation

Virginia: See Coalition of Taxpayers

Washington Institute for Policy Studies
P.O. Box 24645
Seattle, WA 98124
(206) 938-6300
(206) 938-6313 FAX
jcarlson@wips.org

Washington Research Council
1301 5th Ave., Suite 2810
Seattle, WA 98101
(206) 467-7088
(206) 467-6957 FAX
71550 2021@compuserve.com

ABOUT THE AUTHORS

ROBERT BENNINGTON

Robert Bennington has had varied career experiences ranging from law enforcement to sales trainer and motivational speaker for a national medical supply company. Currently he is president of the National Audit Defense Network, which is composed of former IRS agents, auditors, and tax attorneys who represent taxpayers during IRS audits. As a nationally recognized expert on taxation issues, Robert has spoken as a guest expert on media ranging from CNN and the Jim Lehrer News Hour to G. Gordon Liddy and Michael Reagan.

Robert received a Bachelor of Arts Degree from the University of Southern Florida; he has been a Las Vegas resident for more than eight years, and is married and has two children.

CORT W. CHRISTIE

Mr. Christie has been active in the fiscal world throughout his life, starting with his family's business, which was established in 1901. He was the youngest Financial Consultant ever hired in his region by Merill Lynch and Co. Mr. Christie conducts seminars around the country on entrepreneurial subjects including: Basic Corporation Fundamentals; Advanced Corporate Strategies; Offshore Corporate Strategy Secrets. He is known worldwide for his extensive knowledge of tax strategies, incorporating businesses, and financial success. Christie owns and operates several national enterprises that are experiencing rapid growth. Mr. Christie continues to consult daily with his clients at home and globally on business plans, asset protection, and privacy.

In addition to lecturing on the subject of corporate structuring, Mr. Christie is involved with educating the public about the sometimes hidden facets of the Internal Revenue Service and what it takes to avoid the dreaded tax audit! Many of his feature lectures have focused on tax planning and IRS audit representation.

In addition to *800 Away IRS*, Cort is also the author of *Incorporating In Nevada* and numerous journal and newsletter articles about the IRS and tax strategy. He is a graduate of the University of Minnesota with a Bachelor of Arts in Finance, and currently resides in Las Vegas with his wife, Jennifer, and their two young children.

HOW TO BECOME A MEMBER

TYPE OF MEMBERSHIP

☐ Individual ☐ Business ☐ Combo
1 year / $397 1 year / $497 1 year / $847

CORPORATIONS, PARTNERSHIPS & TRUSTS

Business Name: _____
Federal ID#: _____
Street Address: _____
City/State/Zip Code: _____
Phone: (___) _____Fax: (___)_____

INDIVIDUAL MEMBERSHIP

Name: _____
Spouse (for Joint Returns): _____
Social Security #: _____
Street Address: _____
City/State/Zip Code: _____
Work Phone: (___) _____Fax: (___) _____
Home Phone: (___) _____

METHOD OF PAYMENT
(payable to National Audit Defense Network)

☐ VISA ☐ MASTERCARD ☐ DISCOVER ☐ AMEX ☐ CHECK

CARD #:_____EXP. DATE: _____

SIGNATURE: _____

CHECK #:_____AMT. $_____CHECK DATE:_____

HOW TO ORDER THIS BOOK

To receive additional copies of 1-800-AWAY-IRS, call toll-free
1-800-280-8659 or mail a request with $22, including $3 for shipping
and handling, to address below.

SEND MEMBERSHIP APPLICATION AND/OR BOOK ORDER TO:

National Audit Defense Network,
5300 West Sahara, Suite 100, Las Vegas, NV 89102
or fax a request to (702) 889-8825
or call 1-800-280-8659 (in Nevada call (702) 889-8820)